Margaret Deland

The story of a child

Margaret Deland

The story of a child

ISBN/EAN: 9783743308909

Manufactured in Europe, USA, Canada, Australia, Japa

Cover: Foto ©ninafisch / pixelio.de

Manufactured and distributed by brebook publishing software (www.brebook.com)

Margaret Deland

The story of a child

THE STORY OF A CHILD

BY

MARGARET DELAND

AUTHOR OF "JOHN WARD, PREACHER," "SIDNEY," "FLORIDA
DAYS," "THE OLD GARDEN, AND OTHER VERSES"

Heaven lies about us in our infancy
WORDSWORTH

BOSTON AND NEW YORK
HOUGHTON, MIFFLIN AND COMPANY
The Riverside Press, Cambridge
1892

Copyright, 1892,
By MARGARET DELAND.

All rights reserved.

The Riverside Press, Cambridge, Mass., U.S.A.
Electrotyped and Printed by H. O. Houghton & Co.

To the dear Memory of

N. W. C.

In recollection of a happy childhood

THE STORY OF A CHILD

I

"MY own opinion is," said Mrs. Dale, "that he heard they were coming to Old Chester again, and he felt that his presence would be an embarrassment to her, and so went away. Very properly, I 'm sure; it shows very nice feeling in a person like Mr. Tommy."

"Well, perhaps so," Mrs. Wright agreed; "but I don't know why he should shut up his little house, and go away, dear knows where, just because she is to be in Old Chester for the summer. Suppose he was foolish when she was here before; I don't know but what it shows a little conceit on Mr. ——, on his part, to think that his presence makes any difference to Jane —

I mean to her." Mrs. Wright corrected herself nervously, glancing at the little figure curled up on the steps of the porch. Mrs. Dale raised a cautioning finger. "Children do understand things in the most astonishing way," she said in a low voice.

"Oh, yes," Mrs. Wright said quickly; "I didn't mean to mention names, I'm sure. But it is so awkward to have the apothecary shop shut up, and have to go to Willie King's for one's medicines, all because Jane Temple — Oh, dear me!" ended Mrs. Wright, blankly.

"She didn't hear you," Mrs. Dale assured her; "it's almost her bedtime, and she will go in, in a few minutes. But do be careful, dear Susy."

Mrs. Wright, who despite her forty-five years was still in the bubbling inconsequence of youth, said nervously, "Oh, my gracious, yes! I didn't mean to; only, the Temples haven't been in Old Chester for four years, and I'm sure that is time enough for him to have forgotten that he was ever so foolish as to think of — of *her*," said Mrs. Wright, swallowing the name; "and I'm sure she never encouraged him!"

"Of course not," Mrs. Dale agreed.

"They are talking about Mr. Henry Temple's sister," the child on the steps reflected; "and they are talking about Mr. Tommy Dove going away and leaving his house all shut up. They have to talk about those things because they are grown up."

In her heart she pitied them, but not too deeply to disturb the joy of that delicious melancholy that a child feels in the summer twilight. She put her head down on her arm, and looked up into the branches of the locust-trees, standing, sentinel-like, on either side of the porch. She followed with her eyes the curious outlines of the gnarled and twisted limbs, as they were drawn against the violet of the evening sky. She knew those outlines well; they met and crossed in a way that suggested the arm and clenched hand of an airy giant imprisoned by the growing branches. She had, long ago, fashioned a story to suit the tree picture: She said to herself that when her grandfather died this hand was stretched out to rob her of her grandmother, too, but that the wrinkled branches of this friendly tree had caught it and held the giant fast; when the wind blew she could hear him whispering and complaining, but the faithful tree still kept him a prisoner, so that he could do no harm. The thought that he might ever escape made her shudder; it occurred to her that it would be wise to do something to keep the tree friendly; perhaps water it every evening?

Such plans led her far away from the talk of the grown people. She did not hear Mrs. Wright say that if only "he" had been in a different walk of life she would have been glad enough to have had "her" marry him. "Her life in her brother's family can't be very happy," said Mrs. Wright; "her sister-in-law is such a wretched invalid that she, poor dear, has to give herself up to the housekeeping and to those two children. She ought to have a home of her own; of course she would be lonely, but an unmarried woman must expect to be lonely.". Mrs. Wright said this with as much severity as a plump woman can; she tried to have Christian charity for every one, but, being happily married herself, she found it hard to excuse Jane Temple's single life.

"Yes," Mrs. Dale admitted, briefly, and then added, "but it is better to be lonely than to wish to be alone. If she had married a man so different from herself, she might have come to that." The child, sensitive to the change in her grandmother's voice, looked up, and her little forehead gathered in anxious wrinkles; she thought she would like to take Mrs. Dale's hand, and kiss it, and say, "Don't be sorry!" She listened for some comment from Mrs. Wright, but none came. How still they were, these two, sitting in the darkness! The full skirt of her grandmother's silk dress looked as though it were carved out of black marble, and above it glimmered whitely the old solemn face that she loved and feared; Mrs. Wright's comfortable form seemed to melt into mystery; and suddenly, as she looked at the two motionless figures, all the intangible dumb terrors of childhood began to rise in her throat. Oh, if they would only speak; if she could hear some other sound than the high faint stir of the leaves above her, and far away, below the terrace, the prolonged note of a cicada!

"Suppose," she said to herself, her eyes widening with fright, "suppose that all of a sudden grandmother's head and Mrs. Wright's head were to roll off, and roll down the steps, right here, beside me!" Her breath caught in a sob of terror. The vision of the rolling heads frightened her to the last point of endurance; she could not trust her voice to say goodnight, but darted down the steps, and ran, her knees trembling under her, along the path to the back of the house. She knew that the servants would be in the kitchen; yawning, very likely, over the good books Mrs. Dale provided for their edification, or rocking and sewing in stolid comfort, but alive — speaking! In her rush along the dewy path, the child had a ghastly thought of a dead world, herself the only living thing in it; but that was followed by the instant reflection, that under those circumstances she might walk into the queen's palace and put on a crown; this thought was so calming that when she reached the women she had no desire to throw herself into Betsey's arms, as she had planned to do, declaring that she would be a good girl forever afterwards. This promise had seemed to Ellen necessary as a bribe to Something; but, her passionate fright over, the impulse faded, and she was content to pin Betsey's shawl around her waist, and walk up and down the kitchen with a queenly tread, absorbed in visions of future, if solitary greatness. The two ladies upon the porch were rather relieved by her flight, though Mrs. Wright checked her kindly gossip long enough to say, "Why, what is the matter with Ellen?"

"She has gone to tell Betsey to put her to bed, I suppose," Mrs. Dale said. "Dear me, Susy, she is a great care! I wish she were like your Lydia,—quiet and well-behaved. I often think I'm too old to train a child; and she is very like her mother! Poor Lucy was not brought up according to our ideas, you know."

"She reminds me of Dr. Dale, sometimes," said Mrs. Wright, who was conspicuous in Old Chester for always saying the wrong thing.

Mrs. Dale's face hardened. "I only wish she may grow to be like my dear husband in — in amiability."

"Oh, dear me, yes!" cried Mrs. Wright, with an exuberance that betrayed her. "Dear Dr. Dale!"

Mrs. Dale bowed her head.

The thoughts of both these women were on Dr. Eben Dale, — one with honest pity, the other with the scorch of mortification and anger. He was dead, the brilliant, weak old man, — dead, and escaped from his wife's fierce rectitude. In their youth she had harassed him with the passionate spur of exacting love, but latterly that had been exchanged for contempt. And then he died. No one guessed her grief, covered as it was by bitterness, and yet no one knew her fear of that joyous and imaginative temperament which had made it easy for him to go wrong, and which she saw repeated in her grandchild.

When Mrs. Wright said that little Ellen was like her grandfather, Mrs. Dale's heart contracted; she lost her interest in Jane Temple's affairs; she began to examine her conscience as to whether she was doing her duty to the child. It seemed to her that her husband was looking at her from Ellen's eyes, — looking and laughing, as though he and she took up the old quarrel again.

"Like her grandfather!" Mrs. Dale's thin old hands clasped each other in a tremulous grip. "Oh — no — no!" she said to herself. "Oh, if my Heavenly Father will only give me grace to train her for Him!"

II

OLD CHESTER is a hundred years behind the times; so, at least, it is assured by its sons and daughters, who have left it to live in the great world, but who come back, sometimes, for condescending visits to old homes. The town lies among the rolling hills of western Pennsylvania,— hills which have never echoed with the scream of the locomotive, but are folded in a beautiful green silence, broken only by the silken ripple of little streams which run across the meadows or through the dappled shadows of the woods.

There is not much variety in Old Chester. The houses are built in very much the same way: broad porches; square rooms on either side of a wide hall that runs from the front door to the back; open fireplaces like black caverns under tall wooden mantelpieces. In all the gardens the flower-beds are surrounded by stiff box hedges, and all the orchards are laid out in straight lines.

The people are as much alike as their houses: they read the same books, go to the same church, train their children by the same rules, and are equally polite, reserved, and gently critical of one another.

Perhaps the most striking thing about the village is the way in which the children are brought up. In Old Chester young persons are supposed to be seen, and not heard; they are taught that when they have the privilege of being in the company of their elders and betters it is to profit by example, and be grateful for advice. Thus they early perceive that their opinions are of no importance, and need not be expressed; a perception which adds greatly to the comfort of grown persons.

In spite of this admirable system, there has been more than one black sheep in the village. There was Eben Dale himself, although his youth dated so very far back that perhaps his maturity should not be quoted against Old Chester. Henry Temple, too, had not turned out well — except in a worldly way; and the worldly way was of small importance in Old Chester. Indeed, without quite putting it into words, the village felt a little lack of gentility in Henry's undoubted wealth; and that, added to his change in politics, and his indifference to church matters, and his willingness to live in the great world instead of the village, was enough to make Old Chester say that he had "not turned out well." "Such a pity that his father was so lenient with him!" the people said; and waited calmly for some Nemesis to overtake him. It being a peculiarity of Old Chester to believe that an overruling Providence agreed with it in questions of desert.

There had been one instance of over-severity in the village, but only one, and that not among the families of importance. This was in the case of Mr. Tommy Dove, the apothecary. His mother had ruled him with an iron rod until his forty-seventh year; then death pushed her from her throne, and left Mr. Tommy free, except, indeed, for the restraint of tenderness, which death, kindly but untrue, left in her place. Yet he soon rallied into self-reliance; "remarkably soon," Old Chester commented disapprovingly; for, within three months after her death, he took advantage of his liberty to go gadding about the world, leaving his patrons to get their medicines where they might.

Dates were remembered chronologically in the village: "Dr. Dale gave up practice the winter that the first Mrs. Drayton died;" — "Henry Temple voted the wrong ticket the year there was a snow-storm when the apple-trees were in bloom;" and "Mr. Tommy's first ill-regulated action in mysteriously leaving town took place the summer that Henry Temple and his family were here."

Mr. Tommy was hardly important enough to gossip about, but Mr. Temple was; and, incidentally, his children were discussed; for spoiling Richard and Euphemia was another of his sins. Not even his sister's efforts to train them could make up for his shocking carelessness, people said. That Miss Jane did her best was plain enough; but Miss Jane was gentle and timid and self-distrustful, as every unmarried woman should be; and the children, unfortunately, were like their father, headstrong and self-satisfied. So how could she discipline them?

Beside, the summer of the Temples' first visit, — the summer Mr. Tommy had disappeared, — Miss Jane had a small happiness and interest of her own, which no doubt claimed the thought that might have been given to Effie and Dick. It was not a very exciting happiness; only a pleasant talk now and then with Mr. Dove, or an occasional call from him in those fragrant summer evenings. They would sit alone, these two elderly persons, in the dimly-lighted drawing-room, hearing a murmur of talk in the library across the hall, or starting with a fright which neither of them understood, if a door opened and closed, or if Mr. Henry Temple's voice was heard in the hall. Mr. Dove had dared to give Miss Temple a bunch of flowers, once; and once, too, had embarrassed and touched her by bringing her a little green crape shawl which had belonged to his mother. It was all very harmless and very pleasant; when, suddenly, Old Chester learned with astonishment that its apothecary had gone! Of course the reason could not long be concealed: Mr. Tommy, the village declared, aghast and disapproving, but grateful for a bit of gossip, — Mr. Tommy had made love to Jane Temple!

But that was four years ago, and Mr.

Tommy, who returned as soon as the Temples left the village, had behaved so properly ever since that his presumption was not remembered against him, until now, when they were coming back again, a second abrupt and mysterious departure brought it all to mind.

"So foolish in Mr. Tommy," every one said, severely, and looked at Jane Temple to see how she took it. Miss Temple took it calmly; there was a quick, surprised glance at the closed house standing in its neglected garden, and a little heightened color in her cheek when she went to Willie King's to have one of Mrs. Temple's prescriptions filled. Perhaps she was too busy for any embarrassment, or regret, or wonder; her sister-in-law's health was an absorbing anxiety; Effie's lessons had to be looked after; Dick needed her to keep his fishing-lines in order; Mr. Temple was so good as to let her be of use in his literary work, to the extent of copying manuscript for him. Beside, there was a certain occupation in the mere delight of being back again in her old home, among old friends. This quiet, old-fashioned living which afforded Mr. Henry Temple much diversion was dear and sacred to her. There was nothing droll to her ears in being called a "girl;" it gave her a pathetic happiness to have Mrs. Dale apologize for speaking of a delicate subject in her presence. "I forgot you were here, my dear," Mrs. Dale said, and Miss Jane blushed, properly and prettily, and felt comforted and cared for. She knew more of the great, indifferent, vulgar world than Mrs. Dale ever dreamed of, but she cast down her eyes unaffectedly when the older woman apologized for speaking of the misconduct of a village girl. She wished she might draw Dick and Effie into this tranquil life which so refreshed her. She looked at these two young persons, and pitied them because they did not know Youth. Here, in Old Chester, how carefully Youth was guarded! It was still protected and considered when maturity had set its mark about soft lips and gentle eyes. It was done by snubbing, Henry Temple said, but Miss Jane never felt snubbed; she saw only kindly protection in the condescension which so amused her brother, and her elderly, starved heart basked in it with great content. She was so modest, so grateful, that her friends were pleased to say of her that Jane had no "airs." This most satisfying praise could not be given to the rest of the Temple household; the two children were especially "airy," and "snubbing" became a matter of duty to all thoughtful persons. "That unfortunate Temple child," Old Chester said, in speaking of Effie, "must really be reproved." The reproof was only the rebuke of a grave manner and a discreet indifference to what she said and did, but it astounded and irritated the child. To hear herself addressed, on the rare occasions when she was noticed, as Euphemia, instead of Effie, — for Old Chester did not approve of nicknames, — filled her with childish rage.

"My name's Effie; I don't like to be called Euphemia," she always retorted glibly; and she gave her opinion of Old Chester, in this connection, with great freedom and force to Ellen Dale.

"How queer and old-fashioned everybody is here," she said, "and how funny to be called Ellen; it's such an ugly name! Why don't you make your grandmother call you Nellie?"

"Make" her grandmother! Ellen, who was really a year older than the fine young lady who addressed her, shivered; yet there was no Old Chester child so quickly influenced by Effie Temple as she.

All the children had received Effie with admiration, and even a little fright. Ellen and her dearest friend, Lydia Wright, talked about her in lowered voices. They felt vaguely that there was something naughty in thinking too much of the strange little girl, whose hair hung over her eyes and waved loosely about her shoulders, who possessed two rings, and who never wore aprons. One morning, soon after Effie's arrival in Old Chester, Ellen whispered to Lydia behind her spelling-book, at school, that if she would come down to the fence of the east pasture that afternoon, she would be there, — "and tell you something about *her*," she ended mysteriously.

Lydia opened her round eyes very wide, and shook her brown curls. "May be my mother won't allow me to go down to the east pasture, Ellen."

"But if you just happened to be walking there," Ellen tempted, "an' I happened to be walking on my side of the fence? it is n't like visiting; I guess we need n't ask leave."

"Well," said Lydia doubtfully.

"If you *should* be there, and you should bring your sewing, I'd do it for you," Ellen enticed; "only, of course, may be *I* won't be there."

"Well," said Lydia again, but with more firmness.

"Mother did n't say I must n't," she assured herself, when, in the afternoon, silencing her conscience with casuistry learned from her friend, she ran across a sunny meadow, and through the deep grass of an orchard, and reached the east pasture. Two poplars, one on either side of the fence, dropped flickering shadows through the sunshine, and their smooth trunks offered a comfortable support to any one who climbed up and sat on the fence, as Ellen was doing now.

"Why!" said she, affecting vast astonishment. "Where are you going? Won't you stop a minute and talk?"

"Why, Ellen," faltered the other, "you said" —

"I *happened* to be walking along here," Ellen interrupted, frowning, — it was so stupid in Lydia to forget to make believe; "I saw you coming, and I waited a little while. It is n't visiting."

"Oh, no," Lydia assented weakly. "I — I brought the handkerchief to hem, Ellen. You said you would," she ended, with a confused air.

"Oh, I don't mind doing a little for you," Ellen returned, in an obliging manner; she ignored the arrangement, but she did not ignore the work.

Lydia reached the handkerchief up to her, and then climbed on the fence and settled herself comfortably against her poplar. Ellen whipped a thimble out of her pocket and began to sew very fast. "She's coming to our school until it closes, and when it does, she is to have a governess."

"Oh!" cried Lydia. There was no need to say who was coming. To the two children Effie Temple was the only person of importance in Old Chester.

"She doesn't want to," proceeded Ellen. "I heard grandmother tell Mrs. Drayton so. Grandmother said it showed how she was brought up, that anybody knew or cared what she wanted. Grandmother said she was *spoiled!*"

"Oh, my!"

"But she's coming, any way. And, Lydia, do you know, she talks French!" Lydia was speechless. "They're coming to tea to our house to-morrow night, and she's coming. And grandmother said I might have my tea-set on the table on the side porch,— just Effie and me. I wish grandmother would invite you."

"Won't she?" Lydia asked anxiously.

"No," Ellen assured her, sighing. "I guess I'll go home now and fix my tea-set for to-morrow night. I wonder if she'll like to play hollyhock ladies, or hear stories? Do you suppose she'll like stories? I'll tell her lots. I'll tell her what happened to me when I was a little girl and was sick."

Lydia knew this story well, but she could not resist asking for it again, and listening with delightful shudders, while Ellen, cheerfully, her hands clasped around her knees, staring up into the branches above her, related, circumstantially, and with that pride in illness which children feel, how she had taken lots of medicine, and got worse, and worse, and worse, and *worse;* and then at last they thought she was dead; and she was put into a coffin and buried, — here she paused to quake with terror, not at her bold untruth, but at the picture she had conjured up, — and how she had "escaped," — and thus, and thus. Neither child believed this marvelous tale, but it was true to both. Midway in her fiction Ellen stopped to say, "Oh, Lydia, do you know any French at all?"

It was not often that Lydia occupied the proud position of instructor to Ellen, so it was a happy moment when she said, "Yes, I do; I know 'How do you do, this morning?' My brother told me."

"Oh, tell me," Ellen begged; and Lydia generously said something which sounded like "Coma-voo port ah voo, set mattan."

Her pleasure at giving Ellen information almost made her forget the vague and gnawing consciousness that she had done wrong in coming out without permission.

III

THAT tea-party was an event in Ellen's life. To begin with, she had a quarrel with Betsey Thomas, who was dressing her.

"I don't want to wear a white apron; it's too babyish. I won't! So there!"

"You will," Betsey assured her briefly, holding out the hated garment. Ellen stamped and opened her lips for some outcry, but there was a sound in the hall outside the door, and she only drew a sobbing breath and waited; she knew that slow rustle of her grandmother's dress. As for Betsey, she hailed it with delight.

"If you please, ma'am," she said, as

Mrs. Dale entered, "Ellen won't put on her apron."

"Grandmother, I don't see why I should wear an apron. I'm going on twelve, and Effie does n't have to, and" —

"That is enough, Ellen."

Mrs. Dale's hair, soft and white as spun silk, was caught back by little tortoise-shell combs, and fell in three short, thick curls on either side of her face; she wore a turban, made of snowy muslin, and the bosom of her black satin gown was filled with the same soft whiteness, crossed in smooth folds and fastened with a small pin in a silver setting. Her delicate old hands were covered with rings, most of them with strands of hair beneath dull glass. She looked at her little granddaughter critically. "Tie her hair back with a brown ribbon, Betsey Thomas," she said, and Ellen involuntarily put up her hands to protect the pink band which held her straight brown locks smoothly in place. Ellen wore her hair, as did all Old

Chester little girls, parted in the middle and cut short behind her ears. It was so thick that it made her head look like a mop.

Even Betsey regretted the order about the pink ribbon. "She wants," the maid explained afterwards to the cook, "to make that child just as old-fashioned as if she was fifty, I do declare! And that little Effie, all dressed up, and banged and all that. There! I did pity our Ellen."

Ellen pitied herself, but submitted to the brown ribbon with only a quiver of her little red upper lip. She gave a despairing glance in the long glass, and saw a small, sturdy figure in a green frock,— a frock reaching nearly to her ankles, and made very simply, with only a frill in the neck and sleeves for trimming; she saw the white dimity apron with tabs pinned up on each shoulder; then, rosy cheeks, big troubled eyes, and the brown ribbon tying back the straight, silken, brown hair. That straight dark hair was Ellen's greatest cross. Many, many times she had added to her prayers the petition that it might grow light and curly, or that she might own a frizzled yellow wig; and she had painfully eaten many crusts of bread, having been told by some deceitful disciplinarian that to eat crusts would make her hair curl. Perhaps she would have been happier had she known that Mrs. Dale, watching that glance into the mirror, was saying to herself, "How much better my little Ellen looks than that furbelowed Temple child!" But Mrs. Dale would never have told Ellen that she looked nicely, lest the knowledge should make her vain.

When Ellen saw the "Temple child," with her yellow hair, and her white dress and blue sash, she had a moment of that intense anger which only childhood knows. She grew white, and her grandmother, seeing the change of color, said to herself that she was glad to see the child show a little shyness. Generally Ellen was too modest to be shy, though Mrs. Dale did not make that distinction in her thoughts. As for Effie, she was neither modest nor shy.

"Oh, how do you do?" she said, and took Ellen's limp hand in hers with the most matter-of-fact and grown-up politeness. Then Mrs. Temple spoke kindly to Ellen, and murmured something about her dear dead mother; and Miss Jane kissed her, and said she hoped she would come to see Effie often.

"If grandmother will allow me," Ellen answered, her anger ebbing as she spoke.

"Now, Ellen," said Mrs. Dale, "take your little friend to the side porch. Have you put out your tea things? Euphemia, you and Ellen are to take tea on the side porch."

Ellen was quite joyous by this time, and took her guest's hand with smiling haste. Effie looked blank. "Are we to go away?"

"Oh, we are going to have a good time; we're going to have tea all by ourselves. Come, we must set the table!"

There was a bubble of happiness in her voice. She had forgotten the brown ribbon, and the plain frock, and her wrath. One could not be angry when one could drink tea on the side porch, where the jasmine was blooming on the lattice, and where one had one's own china dishes, and small cakes baked to fit them!

Effie stared at her. "Does your grandma make you set the table? How horrid! We have servants. I thought your grandma was rich?"

"Rich?" said Ellen. "I don't know. Don't you think it's fun to put out your own china? It's mine, you know. See! isn't that teapot pretty?"

Effie admitted that it was; but she looked at it with a bored irritation. "How queer, not to go to supper with the grown people," she said.

The table on which Ellen spread her cloth was really only a wide bench at one end of the porch. It was so low that the children sat on hassocks instead of chairs.

Through the long hall, from the front porch, they could hear the voices of the company; but here all was quiet, save for their own chatter.

"Let's get some roses for the table," Effie suggested, beginning to be interested.

"Oh, yes!" cried Ellen, and then hesitated. "But I didn't ask grandmother."

"Do you have to ask? Why, I should just tell the gardener to get me bushels, if I wanted them."

"Would you?" said Ellen wistfully. "I have to ask."

"Well, I think that's perfectly *dreadful*," Effie sympathized, emphasizing her words in a way that was quite new to the other child. Indeed, many things were new to Ellen. By the time the little feast was over she had learned much that she had never suspected. She was told that Betsey ought to call her "Miss Ellen or Miss Nellie; Ellen is awful. I'm going to call you Nellie or Nettie; how would you like Nettie? Ellen is *dreadful!*" She was assured that she looked awfully queer with her hair parted and cut so short, and with no bang, and also that it was funny to wear an apron: although, indeed, she knew that, she said. And then she confided the story of the afternoon.

"I would n't stand it!" cried Effie. "I would n't let anybody rule me that way! I 'd — why, my goodness, I think your grandmother is awfully cruel."

Ellen gasped.

"You poor little thing," Effie went on, "it 's perfectly shameful, the way they treat you. Well, never mind; I 'll take care of you, only you *must* have some spirit. Watch me, and I 'll show you how to act: Here, Betsey! give Miss Nellie some more cake."

Betsey was "that dumfounded," as she told the cook afterwards, that she "did n't hardly know what to say;" what she did say, looking severely at Ellen, was, "Eat your pudding, and don't talk," which Ellen scarcely deserved, being speechless with astonishment. She was thinking to herself, "What will Lydia say when I tell her about it at recess to-morrow?" But she helped Effie to the pudding, and suggested that they should make believe that the little mounds of rice on their plates were mountains, and the brown, soft raisins hidden in them were the bodies of travelers buried in the snow, and they themselves were noble St. Bernard dogs, searching, at terrible risk, to save imperiled lives. To do this, made the simple dessert delicious to Ellen, who, in eating each frozen traveler as soon as he was found, was not disturbed by any sense of incongruity. But she had so far profited by Effie's example that when Betsey reproved her for leaving some rice upon her plate, with the remark that it was wicked waste, and that some poor child would like to have it, she had the courage to retort that she did n't see what good it would do the poor child if she ate the rice.

"So there!" Effie added, to encourage her.

"And from that minute," Betsey Thomas used to say, " I took a dislike to that young one!"

Effie's indignation at her hostess's hard lot was very impressive to Ellen; Lydia had never seemed to be so sorry for her, she thought. But although it was interesting to talk about herself, she felt that politeness demanded that she should entertain her guest, and so, when tea was over, she reluctantly interrupted Effie's sympathy to ask her if she would like to play martyrs.

"Martyrs?" said Effie, with an unflattering readiness to change the subject. "What is it? I don't know; yes. Is it forfeits, or anything like that? I like forfeits, but I don't want to play any old improving game."

"It is n't a game," Ellen explained; "it 's just — martyrs. Lydia and I play it. Come down in the garden and we 'll make them. Do you think you could be a martyr, Effie?"

"Well, you are the queerest girl!" was all Effie vouchsafed to say.

The two children ran across the lawn, and down between the box-edged borders to a group of hollyhocks, standing like slender spires against the yellow sunset. Ellen's face was grave and eager as she chose the flower she wanted, but Effie was not certain whether to be contemptuous or interested.

A splendid crimson blossom was the first one to be picked. "That is the mother of the family," said Ellen, explaining. — A pale rose came next, — "*that*'s the eldest daughter; this white one is a bride, and she has consumption; and this little yellow one is a little girl. Like me."

"Martyrs!" said Effie, with unaffected contempt. "I never heard of anything so silly."

"You wait," Ellen answered mysteriously. She sat down on the grass, and carefully pulling off the furry calyx of each gorgeous blossom, she bent the silken petals back with careful touches, and then, plucking long blades of grass, tied what she called "sashes" about the waist of her floral dolls; after that, a stalk of grass was thrust through each of these high-shouldered ladies, and there were their arms stretched out at right angles. The feathery pistils made stately headdresses for the four little persons who were to die for a principle.

Then the children went back to the house and pushed four matches down into the mossy line between the flagstones of the path, and tied a martyr to each little stake, heaping bits of twigs as fagots about their devoted forms; by that time Effie was as absorbed as Ellen. Ellen told the "story" of the play, but, as Effie was company, she applied the fire; the "torch," Ellen called it. "And they said, 'If you will recant,'" Ellen recited, the bride's silvery white robe shivering at the touch of the flame, — "'if you will recant you shall have all the money you want, and a palace to live in.' But the lovely lady shook her head, and said, 'I won't,' and so they burned her up." Ellen's lip quivered as she reached this point in the story. The fresh flowers did not burn well, and their prolonged suffering made her so unhappy that, suddenly, she scattered the tiny brands and rescued them.

"Oh, my!" she said, "I'm glad I did n't live in Bloody Mary's time. I would n't have liked to be burned. I know it's wicked, but I would n't. I tried it, to see if I could, and — I *could n't*," she ended, in a shamed voice.

"How did you try it?"

"Well, I put my hand in the candle, like Cranmer."

"Well?"

"I — I took it out again. Oh, I hope there won't be any more persecutions. I get so scared thinking about it!"

"You're the funniest girl!" Effie declared.

Ellen was silent. It seemed to her that

she had been very silly to cry because she had not been able to keep her blistering finger in the candle flame. After a while, she said, in a low voice, "Did you ever read 'Persecutions in Spain'? There's a lot about martyrs in it. It scares me."

"What do you read it for, then?" Effie inquired, not unnaturally; but she could not help being interested when Ellen told her of beautiful nuns walled up alive in dreadful dungeons, and she was constrained to say she would read it some day.

"It would be nice to play walling up," Ellen said meditatively. "We have a brick oven round by the kitchen door; we could crawl in and pretend to be walled up?"

Effie was enchanted with the thought, and the two children hurried, in the fading light, to the old oven. It had a turtle-like back, and stood on three squat brick legs. Bread had been baked in it that day, and it was still faintly warm, and the smell of fresh bread mingled deliciously with the pungent scent of wood smoke. There were traces of ashes about its cavernous mouth, and Ellen pushed in the fire-rake and drew out some charred brands.

Effie had no suggestions to make, but she assented eagerly to all Ellen's plans.

"They used to leave some food for the nuns," said Ellen, "so we must put in a loaf of bread, and a ewer, — it always said in the book a 'ewer' of water. But who will wall us up? That wooden square is the door, and Betsey puts this rake-handle against it, to keep it up when the bread is in. But we can't do that when we get inside?"

"Oh, I'll do it," Effie said: "you get inside, and I'll do it."

This seemed very unselfish on Effie's part. Ellen hesitated, but the temptation was too great, and she crawled into the open mouth of the oven. Then Effie propped the door in place with the rake-handle, and the martyr, curling herself up to fit the small space, folded her hands upon her breast and composed herself for an ecstasy. "I'll sing a hymn," she called out in a muffled voice, — "the martyrs always sing hymns. But I think I'll eat my bread first." She crammed some bread into her mouth, and continued, dramatically; "I must save this bread — I must make it last as long as I can! but I will never recant! Never!"

Effie really shuddered at the tone, and was about to tear open the tomb, when, unfortunately, Betsey Thomas appeared, to tell Ellen that it was her bedtime; Betsey cried out, and scolded, and pulled the ash-covered Ellen from her martyr's grave and into the house, to her intense mortification and anger.

"You go right straight to bed!" said Betsey. "My! just look at you! Well, you can't go on the porch to say goodnight. I'll tell your grandmother; see if I don't, you naughty girl, you!"

In the midst of the tirade Effie slunk

away, and Ellen battled with the servant alone. But in the end she went upstairs to bed, and cried, and thought of what Effie had said of the hardness of her life, and prayed a great deal, with that bitter piety which is a form of resentment and is not confined to adolescence. She looked at her arm, which Betsey had griped with plump fingers while expressing forcible opinions, and saw a faint red mark. She decided to show this mark to her grandmother, but was dismayed to see that the redness was disappearing, and so pinched it a little, that it might bear witness to Betsey's behavior.

As she lay in her little bed, looking out at the fading sky, where suddenly, between the branches of the pear-tree, a star shook and then burned clear, she heard the murmur of voices, and sometimes a little low, pleasant laughter, and she reflected that Effie was there with the grown people, while she — had been sent to bed! — sent to bed and *pinched!* Oh, how miserable she was! How cruel her grandmother was, to oblige her to go to bed at half past eight, like a baby, while Effie stayed downstairs with the company!

Ellen realized that her eyes were wet, and she shut them tightly, so that the tears would show upon her lashes; her grandmother, when she came to her bedside, as she did the last thing every night, should see that Ellen had been crying, and then she would feel badly. Ellen turned over on her back, so that the pillow should not dry the tears, and determined to lie awake to note the effect upon Mrs. Dale. She extended her arm, too, with the sleeve of her night-gown well pushed up above the fading illustration of Betsey's unkindness. The thought of Mrs. Dale's remorse began to soften her, and then— But it was morning, and Betsey was saying, "Come, get up, Ellen, or you'll be late for worship." And all the room was full of sunshine, and it was not until an hour later that she remembered her wrongs.

IV

THE friendship between Ellen and Effie grew very rapidly, in those pleasant summer days; they saw each other constantly, and, as though that were not enough, corresponded by the aid of something that they called a "telegraph,"— a string from the window of Ellen's bedroom to the big locust-tree just within Mr. Temple's grounds. At first, Ellen's feeling for Effie had been ecstatic devotion; she knew for at least a week the tremulous pangs of bliss and pain, the rankling stab of jealousy, the spur of the desire for approbation, the impulsive and ingenious flattery of the lover,— all that goes to make up what is called falling in love. And then her idol shattered the idealization with a wholesome squabble, and Ellen came down to commonplace friendship, in which in games and fancies she was first. In the generosity of her imagination, she told Effie of a plan she and Lydia had, of digging up a great stone in the woods, under which Ellen was convinced were buried many Indian warriors, together with bags of gold, tomahawks, and copper spears. It was their intention to dig the boulder up, and then present the buried wealth to their grateful relatives. The skeletons of the Indians Lydia and Ellen were to keep for themselves.

Effie entered cheerfully into the project, but she did not care to dig; and the stone, gray with lichen, and bedded deep in ferns and moss and years of fallen forest leaves, continued to seal the riches in which Ellen firmly believed. Effie would sit under a tree and watch Ellen tugging and straining at a big stick thrust as a lever under one side of the rock, or digging until her face was as crimson as the single columbine that nodded on the great stone's breast. Effie had not a very lively faith in the skeletons beneath the stone, but she liked to hear Ellen talk about them. "Will they be in coffins?" she inquired placidly.

"No," Ellen told her; "they'll be wrapped in *wampum*; that's golden robes, I think; and they'll have necklaces of bear's teeth, and strings and strings of scalps! Lydia and I meant to keep the scalps; but you can have some." She was very earnest; she could fancy so clearly the great moment when the rock should be at last raised from its bed, — she saw it heaving up, rocking, balancing, crashing over, and rolling with tremendous bounds down the hillside; she knew just how the grave beneath it would look: a square hole in the black soft forest earth, fringed with ferns and windflowers; solemn figures lying straight and still within it, figures holding burnished spears, and glittering with gold and gems, and decked with drooping scarlet plumes; a hundred times she had pictured the moment when she should stand looking down at them, while high up, with faint, far sound, the tops of forest trees stirred between her and the blue sky.

As this project involved more or less hard work, Effie liked better the acting out some of Ellen's romances of daring and of love. Lydia, as a third child, would have added much to their games, but Effie did not like her, and so she was left out of all these joys. Ellen no longer urged her to "walk down by the fence in the east pasture;" Ellen's own faithlessness made her say that the disloyalty was Lydia's; but more than that, her former friend seemed very young!

That Ellen and Effie were so much together was pleasing not only to the two children, but to the entire Temple household. Miss Jane had begged Mrs. Dale to allow her granddaughter to be with Effie as much as possible. "Because," she explained, "Ellen is such a dear child, so modest and well behaved, that I am sure her example will be good for Effie."

Miss Jane said this at the first meeting of the sewing-society at which she was present. She and Mrs. Dale were waiting in the church porch after the meeting, watching an unexpected downpour of summer rain. "As soon as the carriage comes, I'll take you home, Jane Temple," Mrs. Dale said; "you can't walk up the hill in this rain." There was something in her voice which made the younger woman redden, and answer in quick excuse, "I suppose no one at home has noticed the storm, and so the carriage has not been sent for me."

"I suppose not," Mrs. Dale agreed dryly. Like everybody else in Old Chester, she blamed Jane Temple because her family neglected her.

"Besides," Miss Temple asserted, "everybody knows I like the rain. No, I don't mind walking, thank you."

"No doubt," said Mrs. Dale; "but it will give me pleasure to have you, my dear, so I hope you will come. I don't know what has happened to Morris; he should have been here five minutes ago."

The two ladies fell into an uncomfortable silence. The rain dripped steadily from the pitch roof of the porch, and fell into the pebbly gutters below with the sharp running chime of little bells; the bare earth under the branches of the fir-trees on either side of the path gleamed with pools, and the grass beyond, growing thick about the gray tombstones, seemed greener every moment.

"It is quite a rain," Miss Jane admitted reluctantly. "Perhaps I had better drive; but will you let me stop and get a prescription filled for sister?"

"Why, certainly," said Mrs. Dale. "You know Willie King has taken Mr. Tommy's place? I suppose you know that Mr. Tommy has disappeared again?" She was careful not to look at Miss Jane.

"So I heard," Miss Jane answered.

"It's very vexing in Mr. Tommy to run away in this fashion," Mrs. Dale went on. "I wanted him to teach Ellen Latin this summer; you know he is quite a scholar in his small way— Ah, here is the carriage. Get in, my dear;" and then, a moment later, "I wonder if your sister-in-law would allow Ellen to have an hour or two a week with Euphemia's governess?"

Miss Jane, whose face had flushed at Mr. Tommy's name, hastened to say that she was sure Mrs. Temple would be glad to make such an arrangement; then she made her little speech about Ellen's influence. And so it came about that Ellen went to Mr. Temple's house twice a week for her Latin, and at least once beside to spend the afternoon with Effie. This, Mrs. Dale felt, was only doing what she could, as a friend of the family, to improve Henry Temple's neglected child. Ellen carried on this missionary work with a zeal which her grandmother never suspected.

On the hill, up which the orchard sloped to the edge of the woods, was a latticed summer-house. It was old, and long ago the rain had painted it a faint, soft gray; there were vines all about it, which almost hid the diamond-shaped windows in its sides, and lilacs and wild cherries crowded so closely around it that any one looking up from the kitchen garden, or even passing through the orchard, would never have guessed that the two children met in it almost every day. And could their conversation on a certain Sunday afternoon have been overheard, Miss Jane might not have been so sure of Ellen's influence upon Effie, and it is probable that not even Mrs. Dale's willingness to be of service to Henry Temple would have made her consent to the intimacy between the children.

"I don't think," Ellen was remonstrating, "that you ought to speak so to Miss Jane."

"I don't care," said Effie, "I won't be ordered around by anybody. I'm not like you!"

The two children were sitting on the steps of the summer-house; they could look down into the orchard, and over the roof of the Dale house, which lay below them. Beyond was the white, dusty turnpike, and the meadows, and then the blue curve of the Ohio River. It was very silent in the orchard; only the faint rustle of the leaves in the woods behind them and their own hushed voices broke the sunny quiet. Effie had said, in answer to Ellen's request that she should hear her say her hymn, "Do you have to learn hymns on Sunday? I would n't be you! Go on: 'Softly now'" —

> "Softly now the light of day,
> Fades upon my sight away;
> Free from care, from labor free,
> Lord, I would commune with Thee."

Ellen's voice sounded as though she were half ashamed.

Effie, scarcely waiting for the last line, closed the book with a bang, and tossed it into her friend's lap. "Aunt Jane wanted to make me learn a hymn on Sundays, and I just told her I would n't. She asked me if I would n't learn one; and I said, 'I can't, I can't, I *can't*, so there, now!' I knew if I did it once, she'd say I could, and then I might have to do it again."

It was here that Ellen made her protest for Miss Jane, but Effie only tossed her head. "Do you think I care what she says? Nobody cares what Aunt Jane says. Why, look here; I'll tell you something about her, — only it's a secret!"

"I'll never tell," Ellen declared.

But she was not much interested; she was too conscious that it was Sunday. Sunday visiting was not approved of by Old Chester, at least among the children, and even the occasional afternoon calls of grown persons were more or less apologetic. That Ellen, who had been allowed to go out into the garden to study her hymn, should have dared to meet "the Temple child," and spend the long, still, sunshiny hours in idle talk, was something that Mrs. Dale would not have forbidden, because it would never have seemed possible.

Before this new friendship came into Ellen's life, her Sunday afternoons, in summer, had had a distinct and happy character of their own. There were always some verses from the Bible to be studied, and a hymn. And so, book in hand, murmuring over and over words which had little meaning in her ears, she wandered about the garden, "getting by heart," as she expressed it, some of the noblest expressions of the spiritual life. Sometimes she stopped to talk to the flowers; sometimes to lay her cheek against the ground, and look through the mist of grass stems, and weave her little fancies about the world of bee, and butterfly, and blossom; not unfrequently she climbed into the low branches of her favorite apple-tree, and "preached, like Dr. Lavendar," to the congregation below her of bending and rippling Timothy. To hear herself talk of piety and obedience gave Ellen all the satisfaction of good behavior; her exhortations were so earnest that she mistook them for feelings,—a mistake incidental, perhaps, to the pulpit. She might stop at this stage to repeat her hymn, and then, still murmuring it to herself, go down below the terrace where the violets grew thick under a larch tree; to sit down among them, and put a little finger under a blossom's chin and look into its meek eye, gave her far more joy than any mere plucking flowers would have done. She was very apt to come to this part of the garden for a certain ceremony which she called "marrying the grass." She would kneel down and tie two stalks of blossoming grass together, and pronounce some solemn gibberish over them, which, she said, was the marriage ceremony:—

> "Now you're married,
> We wish you joy;
> Your father and mother
> You must obey;
> And live together
> Like sister and brother;
> And now kneel down
> And kiss each other."

Ellen never spoke of these fancies to her grandmother, not from any secrecy or reserve, but because of their absolute commonplaceness. If she ever reflected upon them at all, it was to imagine that Mrs. Dale, and everybody else in the world, had the same pleasant thoughts.

Beside her pretty romancing, she had long theological arguments with herself. Mrs. Dale never imagined the religious fogs into which her grandchild wandered, or how again and again she wearied her little brains over the puzzle of personal responsibility. Nor did she ever fancy the heartache with which sometimes, romancing over, the child sat down to plan ways and means of showing her grandmother her love, for, she thought, if she could only express that, perhaps Mrs. Dale would kiss and cuddle her, as she had once seen a gypsy mother caress a little swarthy black-eyed child. Swaying to and fro, her head on her knees, her mop of brown hair falling forward about her ears, Ellen agonized over her sins, which she was sure kept her from her grandmother's heart. She thought of things she might do to prove her affection: pick all the flowers in her garden and put them down for Mrs. Dale to walk on; kiss the hem of her dress; climb up to the top of the locust-tree, and hang by her feet from the highest branch to give her grandmother pleasure. She thought of all these things, and many more; and yet, somehow, her little, crowding, impetuous love remained unspoken.

The meetings with Effie in the summer-house were, in a certain way, of a healthier character than such dreams; if only they had not been stained by the consciousness of Mrs. Dale's disapproval!

And here, on this still July Sunday, the two children were. Ellen's hymn-book was open on her knee, and she had silenced her conscience for a moment by thinking that she would say to her grandmother, in a casual way, " I saw Effie this afternoon, as I was walking in our orchard, and I asked her to hear me say my hymn." The prospect of confession lightened her heart, and, the hymn repeated, made her stay on to hear the secret that Effie promised. " I 'll never tell," she urged.

"Well," began Effie, edging a little closer to her friend, "you know Mr. Tommy ? I mean the apothecary man." Ellen nodded. "Well, you know how he went away, the last time we were in Old Chester, — oh, years, and years, and years ago, when I was a little girl — and nobody knew where he 'd gone, and he never came back until after we went to town ; and he's gone away this summer again, and nobody knows where he is ? "

"Yes," said Ellen, but she was disappointed. Grown-up people did not interest her, and beside, there was nothing secret so far. "Everybody knows that," she said.

"But nobody knows why he went," Effie proceeded, "except me. It was aunty!" Ellen looked puzzled. "Goose!" cried Effie. "He was in love with her!"

A little more color came into Ellen's rosy cheeks. "Effie, Betsey Thomas says it isn't nice for little girls to talk about — *that*."

Effie laughed shrilly. "Why, I'm eleven months and two days younger than you, and I've been in love myself."

"Oh, Effie!"

"Yes, I have. Well, I am now, too. He's — oh, he's perfectly lovely. He has a market on the avenue, about three blocks away from our house. And he's as big — oh, twice as big as papa. He wears a white apron in the shop, and he's just lovely. And I used to be in love with my cousin, John Lavendar. We were engaged. He gave me a pressed rose, and

I wore it around my neck on a black silk thread; and I gave him a pressed pansy, and he kept it in his watch. We were going to be married when we were fourteen, and we were going to have six children, three girls and three boys. That was when we were engaged. But I told him I didn't want aunt Mary Lavendar for a mother-in-law; she's cross, and I hate cross people. And then he got tired of me," she ended cheerfully. Ellen was speechless with interest. "I wasn't mad; I was tired of him, too. I'll tell you how it was. We were playing croquet, and a little girl, — I think she's a relation of his, her name's Rose, — she came walking along with her nurse. My! she was so little; she wasn't more than four. And John said, 'Effie, if Rose was a little older, she'd do for me, wouldn't she?' And I said, 'Well, she'll get older, and I think I like her brother better than you, so let's change.' So we changed."

"Are you engaged to her brother?" Ellen inquired with anxiety.

"Oh, no," Effie said pensively. "I saw the marketman then, so I did n't care for Rose's brother. But this was the way it was about aunty. Mr. Tommy fell in love with her, and he *proposed.* I know, because I heard papa tell mamma that he came in and found him proposing to aunty. Just think! I wonder what he said? 'Will you be mine?' I suppose. But papa, he would n't allow such a thing, of course. Mr. Tommy, just an apothecary, you know, and to fall in love with my aunt! And any way, she can't ever get married; she has to take care of us. Well, papa sent him off, I tell you! Papa was awfully mad. I peeked in the door, and saw him. And then Mr. Tommy *ran.* I saw him. He ran and ran, as hard as his legs could carry him. And the next day his house was all shut up, and he did n't come back to Old Chester until we 'd gone away."

"And was Miss Jane mad, too?"

"Aunty? No! That's the joke of it.

She liked him. She thought he'd come back. Nellie, would you rather marry a sailor or a man? I'm going to marry the captain of a Cunarder, so that I can go to sea all the time."

Ellen was horrified. "Effie, it isn't right to talk that way, and on Sunday, too! And — the marketman?"

"As though Sunday made any difference! Goodness, I wouldn't be like you for anything, — being told all the time things aren't right, and being ordered round by everybody. I wouldn't stand it."

Ellen's face flushed. "I can't help it," she said sullenly.

"I'd help it!" Effie assured her.

"How?"

"Well," said Effie, "in the first place, I'd just talk right out. I'd say, 'Grandma, I'm too old to be ordered round, and — and I won't stand it!' And then, if she didn't stop being cruel, I'd run away!"

"Oh, I've thought of that lots of times,"

Ellen said dolefully, "only I don't know where I'd go."

"Have you thought of it? Oh, Nellie! Let's talk about it; let's do it. I'll go, too. I'm tired of living at home, though they are not quite as unkind at my house as they are at your house. I've decided to do something; I'm not quite sure what. I did think of going on the stage, but I don't know but what I'd rather be a missionary. It would be awfully nice to go to Africa and see the Great Desert. I tell you what let's do; let's run away and be missionaries. You know lots of hymns, don't you?"

"Yes," Ellen said with enthusiasm (and added, in her own mind, that she would tell her grandmother that she and Effie had talked about being missionaries). "But we're not very old, Effie?"

"We're old enough to teach the heathen," said Effie piously. "I was confirmed at Easter, so of course it's all right for me. Have you been confirmed?"

Ellen shook her head, and Effie looked concerned.

"Well, perhaps then it wouldn't do for you to be a missionary; but I'd run away, anyhow."

"I hadn't thought of being a missionary," Ellen acknowledged; "I only meant to run away. I used to think I'd take one of the benches on the front porch, and turn it upside down, so it would be a boat, you know. Then at one end I'd put some loaves of bread and a little barrel of water, and maybe a ham. Well, then I'd get it down to the river, and push it in, and go floating off. Pretty soon I'd reach the Mississippi" — Ellen's eyes grew vague with her dream. She saw it all as she spoke, — the yellow water lapping and rippling against the sides of the upturned bench; the green meadows along the shore; the sudden splash of paddle-wheels as, perhaps, some great steamboat passed her, and disappearing among the hills, left, like a drift of melody, the sound of its calliope behind it. "When I got to the Caribbean Sea, I'd find a desert island, and live on it. I'd eat cocoanuts, and breadfruit, and get a man Friday, and some goats. Then I'd send beautiful presents home." Ellen paused to think, not of the difficulties of transportation, but, with bitter joy, of the coals of fire such presents would be to her grandmother. "But perhaps it would be better to be a missionary," she ended.

"'Course it would," Effie assured her; and they began to make many plans.

And when, that evening, after tea, Ellen stood before her grandmother, repeating her hymn, she was much too full of her devout intentions to remember to confess how she had spent her afternoon. She heard Mrs. Dale's comments on the hymn, received her quiet kiss, and was told that she might walk about in the garden till bedtime. Her mind was still intent upon voyages, and desert islands, and converted cannibals, but something in the touch of the soft old hand upon her head stirred the child's heart. Confession rushed to her lips.

"Oh!" she said, flinging her arms about Mrs. Dale's neck, "I love you very much; only I — I " — The tears were in her eyes, and her hot face was buried in the spotless neckerchief.

"There, my dear, there; control yourself, Ellen. Ah, my child, if instead of protestations you would be an obedient little girl, how much more that would prove your love than these foolish outbursts!" Mrs. Dale sighed. Ellen drew back quickly; rudely, her grandmother thought. "Be more gentle in your movements," she said; "do not be so abrupt."

"Yes 'm," Ellen answered, with a sob in her throat. "Oh, how I hate grandmother!" she said between her teeth, as she darted down into the garden. There, below the terrace, she threw herself, sobbing, on the grass that grew deep and soft under the solemn branches of a larch. The check to her impetuous love caused her to forget her own wrong-doing. She said to herself that nobody loved her, and she was very wretched. Little Ellen had the temperament which made it possible to observe her sorrows and measure her emotions; life was always more or less spectacular to her, and she exaggerated her woes for very interest in them. Just now, as she was so ill-treated, she wished she might be very ill and die. It gave her pleasure to fancy her sufferings and the grief of her friends; especially did her mind dwell on the neglected Lydia, whose astonishment and sorrow filled her with a delightful sense of power in being able to produce such an effect.

"Or if I could only be drowned!" she reflected, growing happier each moment. "When they found me in the river, they'd carry me home, and how sorry they'd be!" She closed her eyes and saw her white dress (a white dress is necessary for an effective suicide), — saw her white dress dripping and clinging to her figure, and her long hair (for somehow her hair must be long), — her long hair trailing upon the ground, wet and straight. She thought how pale her face would be, how tightly her eyes would be closed; she reflected, with satisfaction, how Betsey would cry and say she was sorry for all her wickedness; and she thought of Lydia's fright and of her grandmother's repentant grief. At that she involuntarily sobbed, which interested her so much that she began to pity and forgive everybody, and a little later went very happily to bed.

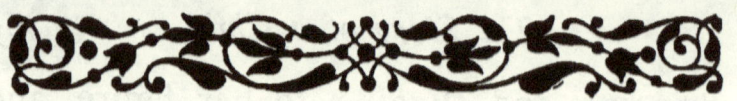

V

EFFIE, who said her head ached too much for study, was leaning out of the school-room window, kicking her toes against the wainscoting, while she waited for Ellen to finish the third declension. "Do hurry up with your old *regibuses*," she called over her shoulder, and a moment later seized Ellen's hand and went skipping from the room, much to the relief of weary Miss Dace.

Effie had a suggestion to make: "Let's go down to the back parlor and play house under the sofa."

"Won't it make your head ache more?" Ellen said, faintly polite, for playing house under the sofa was great happiness.

"No," Effie assured her; "it's only those old stupid declensions that make my head ache. Mamma's awfully afraid I'll overwork; so I always tell her when I think I'm going to have a headache. Isn't your grandmother afraid you'll overwork?"

"No," Ellen said bitterly.

But for once Effie forgot to be sympathetic. "Oh, Nellie," she said, "come look at the idol; somebody brought it from China for papa."

She pulled Ellen across the room, where, in a dim corner, mounted on an ebony pillar, a small bronze Buddha sat on his jade throne. Under oblique and cynical eyebrows, his half-shut, dreaming eyes seemed to stare with strange contempt at the two silent children.

Ellen caught her breath and made a clutch at Effie's arm. The dark god was looking, from under those puffed and drooping eyelids, straight at her.

"Oh, *Effie!*"

"Isn't he ugly?" Effie inquired calmly. "And he's really an idol. He used to be in a temple with lots of little roofs on it, all strung with bells that rung when the wind blew, papa says. And he had things sacrificed to him, — rice and things."

Ellen made no answer. So much came into her mind — scenes from "Little Henry and his Bearer," and various other unpleasant and morbid stories, full of that cheap sentiment which once ministered to childish piety — that she did not find it easy to talk. She said she would not play house under the sofa; and, followed by Effie's reproaches, went home to think about the god. She was very silent at tea, and she lay awake that night for certainly a quarter of an hour, listening to the rain dripping on the leaves of the woodbine about her window, and thinking of the bronze image with his strange still smile. She shut her eyes, and fancied the pagoda with its roofs strung with jangling bells; the hot, white sunshine pouring on the dusty streets; the palm-trees standing like great feathers against the sky, and the figures of people wearing their clothing all wrapped about them, like the paper spills she made for lamp-lighters. Her mind was a jumble of terms — palanquins, rupees, coolies, litters — gathered from the India stories of the Lady of the Manor. The Arabian Nights came in, too, and beautiful slaves and cream tarts and roc's eggs, danced through her mind with bewildering interest. But through all she seemed to see, sitting in the shadows of the temple, with rice and flowers spread before him, and joss-sticks filling the air with heavy fragrance, the dark, squatting figure of the god, smiling cruelly under his tilted eyebrows. She pictured his wonder now at Mr. Temple's drawing-room, his contempt for the two little girls who had stood and looked at him that afternoon, his homesickness for his worshipers, his anger because no sacrifices were offered him. And then came a delightful and terrible thought, a thought which made Ellen say to herself that she was very wicked! After that she fell asleep, but the thought came back to her the next morning, when she opened her sleepy eyes to the sunshine.

"He must miss those sacrifices. There would n't be any harm in doing it, — just for fun. And if all those heathen people think it 's right to sacrifice things to him, why, may be it would be *safer* to?"

More and more delightful did the plan appear of taking some flowers and laying them down in front of him. Yet it was a week before she confided it to Effie.

"Oh, yes, let 's worship him!" Effie agreed with enthusiasm.

But Ellen shrank at the word. "Oh, no, that would be wicked; let 's only pretend."

It was Saturday afternoon, and there was no one at hand to interfere with the strange rites which the two children began to enact, in the back parlor, where, cross-legged upon his jade cushion, the bronze god watched them from under his sleepy eyelids.

It was curious to see the difference in Ellen and Effie as revealed in their relation to their little drama. To Effie, until she grew tired of it, it was a play; to Ellen it was tasting sin, with the subtle, epicurean delight of the artistic temperament.

They made great preparations for their service. They lit the candles in the sconce in the corner where Buddha sat, and then a row of bedroom candles, stolen from the table in the back entry. Ellen made a larkspur wreath, sticking one blue horn into another, until the whole rested in her little palm, a flat, thin crown, just large enough for Buddha's head. Then she brought a dozen of those dark red and deeply sweet roses whose stems are thick with thorns, and put them in his lap. The cool dusk of the room was pierced by thin lines of sunlight, creeping between the bowed shutters of the west windows, and falling in tremulous pools upon the floor. Each line was so clear in the dusk that Ellen chose to think they were golden barriers to the temple, and she must crawl under them to reach the inner court of worship. She did it, solemnly, her little head touching once or twice the slanting sunbeam above her, so that for a moment her forehead and eyes were glorified; then she dropped down on her knees and looked up into the still, dark face. She forgot that she was "making believe;" the god became horribly real to her; she felt the sombre mirth of his cruel eyes following her when she stepped back and forth before him, and the desire to propitiate him grew into actual terror. Effie brought some rice and scattered it in front of the image, and watched Ellen bowing and bending and muttering to herself a little pagan prayer which spoke suddenly in her soul. The perfumes offered some difficulty, but Effie solved it by stealing into her mother's room and bringing down a long green bottle of cologne, which Ellen with a lavish hand sprinkled all about the god.

"We ought to sing, and we ought to have a mat to kneel on," she said, in a whisper, to Effie, who reflected, and then said she would go and get something. A moment or two later she came back with a green crape shawl in her hands.

"It came from China," she explained; "aunty said so. It's just the thing."

Ellen was too absorbed to question the propriety of taking Miss Jane's shawl, nor did she notice that she was staining the delicate "mat" at her feet when, with solemn gestures, she pressed the bottom of the oil-can from the sewing-machine, so that they might offer a libation of oil. "We must sing to him," she said, her eyes wide with excitement; but only Christian words suggested themselves to her. "Heathen god" — she began, "you — you — shall —

'shall reign where'er the sun
Doth his successive journeys run;
Your kingdom stretch from shore to shore,
Till moons shall wax and wane no more.'"

Ellen's eyes were vague with the vision of the words. She saw the yellow sun journeying through the silent sky; she saw water, heaving and swelling, gray and misty, lapping the shores of the world; she saw the thin and melancholy moon, curving like a sickle in dun clouds — "wax and wane no more — no more!" — an end of all things — emptiness — darkness — and this dreadful god unmoved and smiling at the desolation! She began to cry, under her breath.

"What is the matter?" said Effie.

"Hush!" Ellen whispered. "He'll hear you!"

She was standing before Buddha, waving her arms over her head, and saying, in a voice shaken with feeling, the first long words that occurred to her — "Justification — sanctification — predestination!"

She did not know what they meant, but they were out of the catechism, and so were proper to say to a god.

"What are you talking about?" demanded Effie. "Let's play something else. I'm tired of this. Besides, I think it's wicked. Oh, there's aunty! Hide the shawl."

But it was too late. Miss Jane came in, kindly curious, to see that the two little girls were having a happy time. The half-burned candles, the roses on Buddha's lap, the scattered rice, and her own crape shawl, crumpled under Effie's feet, made her silent for a moment with astonishment.

"We were playing heathen," Effie explained hastily. "Ellen wanted to."

"Where did you get my shawl, children?" said Miss Jane indignantly.

"Ellen said we had to have a mat; she put it there. It's an ugly old shawl, any way!"

Miss Jane had lifted it with anxious

hands. "And you have spotted it with something! Oh, Ellen, how could you be so naughty?"

"I'm so sorry — I — didn't know" — Ellen began to cry.

"There, my dear!" said Miss Jane, with remorseful forgiveness. "I didn't mean to be cross, my child; only — I — I — value it very much. A friend of mine gave it to me," — she tried to comfort the child; "it isn't any value in itself, but a friend of mine gave it to me, — a friend whom I have not seen for many years. There, dear, don't cry; we won't say anything more about it." But her voice trembled.

Effie had run away, glad to leave reproof or reproach to Ellen, and glad to escape what the housemaid called "redding up the mess" she had helped to make about the idol. As for Ellen, she went home very soberly. The excitement of "making believe" over, the hideous fact of idolatry presented itself to her mind.

This was the beginning of remorse to Ellen, that most intolerable pain of life. The thought of her sin began to lurk under all innocent pleasures; ready to spring out upon her like some terrible wild beast when she was most unconscious of it, or most forgetful. When she read, or worked, or played, there would come, suddenly, a pang in the breastbone, and the thought of the god.

"Thou shalt not make unto thyself any graven image," poor little Ellen said to herself again and again; "thou shalt not bow down to it or worship it," and then she would follow over and over one line of reasoning which traveled in a circle through justification back to pain.

"If the heathen think it's right to bring rice and flowers and to pray to him, why, it can't be wrong for them to do it. So there is no need to confess to grandmother." She would draw a breath of relief here, and then the stab would come: "But I'm not a heathen! I didn't think it was right."

The accusation and excuse, repeated and repeated, grooved into the child's mind. Once she had a shivering glimpse of a possible wreck of all her little faith; a vague dull pain that grew into the question: "How do we know we are right? We can't do anything more than *think* so, and that's what the heathen do!" But this faded almost as soon as it came, with the reassurance, — "Oh yes; the Bible says so, and so does grandmother," and so far as faith went she was satisfied — but her sin remained. Once, in a passion of pain, she burst out into confession to Miss Jane, who flushed a little, but said, "Oh, Ellen, dear, never mind; I took the spots out."

"I didn't mean that," Ellen whispered, hiding her face on that kind shoulder. "We — we played heathen, you know."

"Well, dear?" said Miss Jane cheerfully.

"Was it — was it — very wicked? Oh, shall I go to hell? Will it be visited

VI

WHEN Miss Jane Temple interrupted the worship of Buddha, she carried the poor little stained shawl upstairs to her bedroom, and then stood and looked at it with eyes that were blurred with tears. It all came back to her: the night that Mr. Tommy had brought this offering and ventured to ask her acceptance of it. She remembered the look of pride and relief that came into his face when she thanked him and said it was beautiful. How cruel it was that, just because she was her brother's sister she could have called such a look into his face! It cut her to the heart that Mr. Tommy had been afraid of *her*. It was not fair that he should have been made to feel she did not care for him because she felt herself better than he; it was not right that he should have thought her proud. Proud? Oh, how happy she could have been in those rooms above the apothecary shop if only duty allowed her to think of her own happiness! Something like resentment came into Jane Temple's face. Her brother's family might have permitted her this one friend. It would not have interfered with her services to them! With a trembling lip, she folded her shawl and laid it back in the bottom drawer of her bureau. She took some rose-geranium leaves from the bunch of flowers on her stand and laid them on it.

After this episode of the god, Effie and Ellen were not so intimate for a little while. Ellen's misgivings lest she had committed the unpardonable sin made her find Effie a less congenial companion, and Effie's self-congratulation on having escaped the scolding she deserved made her more cautious. But the estrangement did not last very long, and the two children were soon confidential again. Effie told Ellen every possible family matter, and it was remarkable how many family matters she knew. She repeated again, dramatically, the story of Mr. Tommy's interrupted proposal, although Ellen, with flaming cheeks, protested that she did n't believe Miss Jane would like it, and she wished Effie *would n't!* She was eloquent concerning Dick's extravagances at college, and how her aunt had given him money to pay his debts, because he did n't want to tell his father. She commented, too, with the alarming frankness of youth, on her father's ill-temper. "Yes," said Effie, "he 's horrid when he 's cross," and then went on to comment on her mother's jealousy of "anybody papa likes; at least, of any ladies," she ended calmly, with that peculiar and discriminating discernment which seems to belong to children and servants.

But for the most part the children talked of the hardships of Ellen's life: that her hair was kept short; that she had to go to bed at half past eight; that she was obliged to do a little sewing every day, hem a frill or backstitch a long seam. Effie, with fluent use of adjectives, pitied her for all these things, but she pitied her most of all because, on Mondays and Tuesdays, Ellen was obliged to make her own bed, and dust and tidy her little bedroom.

"Well," cried Effie, when this cruel fact had been revealed to her, "before I'd be a servant girl!" Ellen had never thought of it in that way before; it had only been "helping." So, at least, she had been told. It had not seemed proper to Mrs. Dale to explain that her real reason for giving the child these little tasks was to teach her that any work was fitting for a lady that could be done with the fine, old-fashioned delicacy which the women of Old Chester brought to every duty.

But Effie left no doubt in Ellen's mind,

that she had been "imposed upon," and was doing a servant's work! Once, very soon after her eyes had been opened to this, Ellen confided her wrongs to Lydia, but was met with blank wonder, which she was quick to resent as "airs;" and the other child's protest, "If mother thinks it right, Ellen, I guess it is," only made her quarrel with Lydia, and "not speak" for several days. She was alert to discover further "impositions," — and as such a search is always rewarded, she found many, and was in a chronic state of injured feelings, a state which expressed itself by sullen looks and neglect of many small and pleasant duties; she grew irritable, with the constant effort to "stand up for her rights." "I don't know what's the matter with our Ellen," Betsey sighed, more than once; "she's awful good, but she's that contrary!" The "goodness" had reference only to Ellen's devotions, which at this time were very marked. Betsey had never been obliged to wait so long with the bedroom candle, while Ellen said her prayers. This was partly for the relief of complaining to her Maker, partly, because she knew she was not behaving well, and was constrained to balance her naughtiness by a little extra religion, and partly because, most often at night, the thought of her idolatry assailed her, and urged upon her works of supererogation in the form of prayers and promises. No doubt much of her naughtiness grew out of these religious impulses which satisfied themselves in visions of good deeds and never crystallized into anything so commonplace as obedience. She was constantly planning great self-sacrifices; heroic bravery, sublime devotion. Such dreams were very concrete: as, for instance, what her conduct would be if the house were on fire; she would rush into the flames, and save — everybody! She gave herself up to such visions one Monday morning; she had left the breakfast-room and gathered some posies for the little blue jug that stood on her dressing-table, and then, forgetting her work in her bedroom, stopped, and got into the swing under the front porch. Ellen was very fond of this latticed inclosure under the high porch, from the rafters of which hung the little swing, that creaked with a dry and dusty rhythm when started by her foot; perhaps part of its charm was a lack of the austere order of the rest of Mrs. Dale's household. It still bore the traces of Eben Dale's light-hearted and inconsequent life; under the rafters above the swing were his long bamboo fishing rods, still with the lines wound in careful spirals from the quivering ends to the stout, silver-clasped handles. As Ellen swung back and forth, they shook and trembled, as they had done, no doubt long ago, on some green bank beside a trout pool. A loop of line from a broken reel hung just above the child's eyes, and through it, in delicious abstraction of great purposes, she looked out, across the sunshine on the side lawn, at the watering-trough in the stable yard, and at the pigeons strutting and cooing on the ridge-pole of the barn.

She was saying to herself, with a swelling heart, "Suppose Betsey Thomas should have small-pox?" And then she went on to reflect upon how tenderly she would nurse her, how bravely, even though her grandmother and all her friends should implore her not to run such a risk. Ah, how they would appreciate her when they saw how noble she was! Very likely she should catch the dreadful disease, and lie for days between life and death; and then how saintly she would be, what hymns she would repeat, what appropriate texts! —

"'It is not death to die,'"

quoted Ellen, her eyes brimming with delightful melancholy, and curling her arms about the ropes of the swing, so that she leaned sideways, comfortably.

"It is not death to die,
  To leave the weary road,
  To join the brotherhood on high" —

"I'd say that," she thought, very sorrowfully. But when she recovered (on the whole, she thought she should recover) she would be very beautiful; not a single scar would mar her face; and how Betsey Thomas would love her!

She paused in planning her saintly revenge long enough to look at the diamonds of sunlight falling through the lattice, and lying on the black, hard earth of the floor; how much nicer it was here, under the porch, than in the parlor! There were garden tools in the corners, and on one side of her playroom, like a long red cornucopia encrusted with crumbling earth, were flower pots of lessening sizes fitted into each other. Ellen could scrawl a large E on the dusty top of an old chest of drawers that stood against the wall of the house; it had scarcely been touched since Dr. Dale had put his flies away, after his last fishing trip. Some of the drawers were half open, and there were packets of flower seeds scattered about in them, and one or two books in yellow paper covers, dog-eared and torn. Ellen had looked at them with a view to improving her mind by reading some of grandpapa's wise books; but alas, they were in French, so that aspiration had been checked. On top of the chest was a china bowl half full of water; Ellen had coiled a dozen horsehairs in it, and was waiting to see them turn into snakes; she kept her paper dolls in an old cupboard fastened above it upon the wall; the sagging doors and rattling shelves could not have given the tissue ladies a sense of security, but Ellen liked to think that they were sheltered there, when she lay in her little bed and heard the wind blow, and caught the murmuring complaint of the giant in the locust-trees. The dolls, she saw fit to say, were in a fort, and they were in great terror lest one of the pythons coiled in the white china tank should crawl out, and up to their little shelter, and open his horrible jaws and hiss at them! Ellen shivered for very horror of the situation — but did not abate her care for the horsehairs, nor put a better fastening on the cupboard door. She liked to think that the beat of wind or rain was the assault of pirates upon the unhappy paper ladies, and the idea of their distress when the door banged gave her all the exhilaration of fright. "If pirates were to break into our house," said Ellen, her foot tapping a diamond of sunshine every time she swung forward, "I would say, 'Sir, kill me, but save grandmother — save'" —

But at that moment Betsey Thomas came hurrying out to look for her. Betsey was busy and not in the best temper; her patience had been sorely tried that morning, because Ellen had seen fit to pour water on the floor when she had been dressing her, for the purpose of discovering whether it would run under her instep. "If it does," said Ellen, holding up her skirts, and dabbling her little bare foot in the water, "it shows I'm very aristocratic, Betsey, and would have had my head cut off in the French Revolution." Betsey had been most unsympathetic, and there had been a tussle, followed by a truce, and now the maid would rather have done Ellen's work herself than get into any discussion with her. But Mrs. Dale had bidden her remind Ellen that her bed was not made, and it was after nine.

Ellen, with a very red face, jumped out of the swing, "I just wish you 'd do your work yourself, Betsey Thomas, so there!" she said.

Betsey looked at her soberly. "Ellen, you ought n't to talk that way, 'deed you ought n't; 't ain't right."

"Well, it is n't your place to tell me what I ought to do, anyhow," Ellen answered.

The chambermaid put her red arms akimbo on her hips and gazed at Ellen with real concern. She was a pleasant-looking maid-servant, with an honest Welsh face and curly red-brown hair; she wore a brown calico gown and a long blue apron with a bib pinned up over her ample bosom. "I don't know what's the matter with you, these days, Ellen," she said. "Come, now; be a good girl, and do your work nice, and please your grandmother."

Ellen made no answer, but she followed the maid upstairs. "You know well enough, Ellen, you ain't behavin' as you ought, nowadays," Betsey went on. "You ought to think what the Good Man likes little girls to be. My! I never see any little girl so sassy as you!"

"Will you be quiet, Betsey Thomas?" said Ellen, turning suddenly upon her.

"Why, Ellen Dale!" cried Betsey, dropping admonition, in personal affront; "you're real impudent. I've a good mind to tell your grandmother!"

Ellen's face was white. "You are a low, mean, miserable, lazy woman," she said in a high, quivering voice, "and if you speak another word more to me I'll kill you!"

This was so awful that Betsey was

shocked into real dismay. " Ellen, I 'll have to tell your grandmother," she said reluctantly.

"I don't care!" cried Ellen. She stamped her foot, stood trembling, flew at Betsey and struck her with all her little might, and then dropped sobbing upon the floor.

Betsey was appalled, but angry also. She turned, and hurried out of the room to find Mrs. Dale.

"Oh, ma'am," she said, coming breathlessly into the dining-room, " Ellen is acting awful! She beat and beat me, ma'am! She acted like as if she was possessed!"

Mrs. Dale was sitting at the head of the long table with as much stateliness as though it were surrounded by guests, instead of merely holding a big basin of hot water, a mop, and glass towels. "Tell me just what Ellen has done," she said briefly. And then listened to the agitated complaint, but made no comment. " You may go now," she said, and proceeded calmly to wipe the teaspoons; she was in no haste to go upstairs. She knew that silence and reflection would be very alarming to Ellen.

Ellen, sobbing on the floor, was straining her ears for her grandmother's step. By and by the waiting grew dreadful; she stopped crying and sat up, pushing her hair back from her eyes. The house was very silent. It seemed to the child as though everything held its breath to hear the reproof which was coming. At last she felt she could not bear it any longer, and she crept out into the entry and looked over the balustrade down into the wide hall. The front door was open, and she could see the hot, bright garden. Stretched out in a strip of sunshine that fell across the threshold into the hall was Rip, the red setter; his glossy side was stirred by his deep breathing, and once a paw twitched, as though he were running in some pleasant dream. Her grandmother's work-table was beside the long sofa, which stood between the dining-room and library doors; there was some knitting on the table, and a book with Mrs. Dale's gold spectacles across an open page, and one of Ellen's white aprons, waiting to be mended. The child felt a quick repentance. How naughty she had been; how good her grandmother always was; and even Betsey Thomas was sometimes kind! She would go downstairs and ask to be forgiven; she would tell Betsey she was sorry; she would say — But at that moment, running lightly up the front steps came Effie Temple. Rip, startled at the sound, rose, yawning and stretching, but Effie did not notice him. She had seen Ellen, and dashed at once upstairs.

"Why, what's the matter?" she demanded. "You have been crying! Why, Nellie, what's the matter?"

Ellen felt the tears stinging again, and all her anger came back with a rush.

"Come into my room," she whispered, and drew the eager Effie into her bedroom. "Oh, Effie, it's awful!" she said in a trembling voice.

"What's awful?"

"I've had such a time with Betsey Thomas; she — she — oh, she talked to me!" Ellen caught her breath in a sob. She did not know whether she was more angry at Betsey, or frightened at the prospect of the interview with her grandmother.

"Oh, is that all?" cried Effie. "I hope you talked back to her?"

And Ellen straightway poured out the whole story. As she talked her courage returned, and her anger burned more fiercely. Effie, sitting on the bed beside her, interrupted her with exclamations of pity and indignation, and when she had quite finished was ready with advice. "I'd make that girl get down on her knees and beg my pardon," she said shrilly. "Gracious, I wish you had some spirit, Nellie!"

"Beg *my* pardon?" said Ellen. "Why, I"— She was ashamed to finish the sentence.

"Of course; and if she should say she wouldn't — well, then I know what I should do."

"What?" asked Ellen faintly.

Effie leaned towards her and whispered something in her ear.

"*Oh!*" said Ellen.

VII

FOR a moment after Effie's whisper the two children looked at each other in guilty silence.

"Oh, would you, *really?*" Ellen said at last, under her breath; but before Effie could answer, the door opened and Mrs. Dale entered. A quick displeasure came into her face at the sight of Ellen's guest, but she only said gravely, "Good-morning, Euphemia," and looked to see the child rise, as Ellen had done; but Effie, as she sat on the edge of the bed, swinging her foot to and fro and playing with her rings, only nodded, with a sheepish look, and said, "Oh, how do you do, Mrs. Dale?"

Mrs. Dale put on her glasses and looked

at her. "Euphemia,"—Ellen caught her breath at the solemnity of the tone,—"I wish to talk with Ellen, so must ask you to leave us."

"All right," said Effie. She rose and shook her skirt, which had wrinkled a little, and gave a careless glance into the mirror as she put on her hat. "Mrs. Dale, may Ellen come over and take tea with me to-night? Mamma said I might ask her," she added impatiently, having learned that such reference to her mother was a necessary formality in Old Chester.

"No."

"Oh, please?" Effie teased, but was dismissed with a decision which ignored her coaxing.

Ellen's face grew red and sullen as Effie left the room, and she stared at the carpet that she might not see her grandmother.

"Now, Ellen, tell me what this means?"

"What what means?" the little girl said in a low voice, still looking at the carpet.

"I am very much grieved, Ellen," Mrs. Dale said, not noticing the question.

No response.

"Betsey Thomas tells me that when she spoke to you about putting your room in order you grew very angry, and — struck her! Ellen, no little girl could do such a thing, unless she had" — Mrs. Dale spoke very solemnly — "unless she had the feeling of murder in her heart. Suppose you had had a knife in your hand when you struck Betsey? you might have killed her! You did not have a knife, but you had the feeling in your soul. Oh, Ellen, I hope you will ask your Heavenly Father to give you a better heart."

Ellen did not reply; her chin quivered, and she felt as though something was beating up in her throat; but her silence was not repentance; it was embarrassment at this talk about her "heart," and her Heavenly Father.

Mrs. Dale sighed; she did not know what to say next. She had been prepared for the fluent and fatiguing excuses of an active imagination, and Ellen's silence confused her; to show affection in such a crisis did not occur to her; she looked at the stubborn little face, and wondered how the child could be so hard. "She does not show a trace of feeling!" thought Mrs. Dale, and sighed. She felt as though she stood outside this one heart in all the world that belonged to her, and sought an entrance in vain. There was a wistful disappointment behind the stern justice in her eyes. "Why have I never gained her love?" she thought; but all she said was that Ellen must spend the rest of the day in her room; at five o'clock, if penitent, she might come downstairs and ask forgiveness. ("Such hardness can be conquered only by severity," Mrs. Dale was thinking sadly.) "I hope," she ended, "that you will remember what I have said about the sin of anger; and that you may remember it, I have made out for you a list of verses in the Bible which speak of anger and passion. You will look them out during the day, commit them to memory, and repeat them to me when you come downstairs at five."

She had written the references on a slip of paper, and putting it down on the white work-table, left the room without another look at Ellen.

She was very much troubled. But it never occurred to her to prick the bubble of the child's naughtiness by treating the matter lightly. She gave to the imagination of a foolish child the deference of conscientious effort, — she took the situation seriously. That Ellen might find it interesting, never occurred to her, for Mrs. Dale could no more have been theatrical than she could have been flippant. "I am too old," she thought, with the painful and pathetic humility of age, "too old to manage children; and I cannot make her love me." Her mouth looked stern and hard. "She is like *him*," she thought; "I never understood him.

The fault must be mine, somehow." Her glasses were so dim she did not see that some one was waiting for her in the hall, until she heard a voice say, "Good-morning, dear Mrs. Dale," and found Miss Jane Temple ready to take her hand at the foot of the stairs.

Now, Miss Jane Temple had come to see Mrs. Dale with a purpose which had only taken definite form that day, although it had been smouldering in her heart for many weeks; she had gone that morning down into the village upon an errand, and had stopped absently at the little gate that shut Mr. Tommy Dove's garden away from the dusty street. The garden was full of the sweet confusion of flowers which had been watched and tended for nearly a generation, and then suddenly left to untrained and untrammeled liberty. There were not many weeds, unless the Johnny-jump-ups, growing outside the borders, could be called weeds; or the portulaca, which had sown itself in the grass from the round bed that lay below the shop window, — half in sunshine, blazing with crimson cups, and half in shadow, with tightly shut and shining buds. White petunias flared broadly between the flagstones of the path, and morning-glories were braided among the prickly branches of the moss-rose; the friendly perennials were more decorous, and kept their old places; the queen-of-the-meadow still lifted her powdery crown, close to the gate; and the hollyhocks and bleeding heart and peonies blossomed, as they had blossomed on the same spot, fifty years before.

Miss Jane Temple, leaning on the gate, remembered how she had stopped there one morning, four years ago, just after old Mrs. Dove's death, to tell Mr. Tommy she was sorry for his grief. She remembered that she had sat on the broad doorstone, which was warm with sunshine, and they had talked of many things. Effie was with her, and the little girl's lip had curled in contemptuous amusement when Mr. Tommy tried to entertain her. The color came into Miss Jane's cheek as she thought of the child's rudeness, and then came the remembrance of that other rudeness to Mr. Dove, on the night when he had tried to tell her that he "cared," — the rudeness of her brother who, entering in the midst of those gentle, stumbling words, dismissed the apothecary with courteous contempt. She remembered how Mr. Tommy dashed into the darkness, leaving his sentence unfinished and never coming back again, even to learn that, although she would not leave her brother's family, she too "cared." At first there had been a faint reproach in her heart because he did not come back, but she had very soon understood it: he wanted to spare her the sight of his mortification. She never supposed that disappointed love could long prey upon him. Miss Jane Temple had had snubs enough in her life to know that mortification leaves a pang more lasting than the serpent's tooth, or than disappointed love.

But she wished that he would come back to this neglected garden, this quiet, shabby house that seemed shrinking behind its lilac and sweet-brier bushes. She wished she knew where he was. In a dozen timid ways she had tried to find out, rather by suggesting the question than by any direct inquiry. And yet, why should she not inquire? Yes, a question, boldly put, need not betray her, and her heart leaped at the very thought of hearing about him.

The mortar and pestle which hung above the shop door, and had long ago parted with any gilding they had possessed, creaked in a puff of wind. "I *will* find out!" she said, and pushed open the gate and went across the deep tangle of the grass to the big thorny bush of yellow Persian roses. She picked one, resolution growing in her face; and then she went at once up the hill to Mrs. Dale's house. "Mrs. Dale will tell me," she said to herself.

But when the two ladies sat down by the work-table in the open hall, and Mrs. Dale, with a little sigh, took up Ellen's apron to mend, Miss Jane began to talk of anything and anybody but Mr. Tommy Dove; the weather, first, and the gardener's anxiety about the drought; her sister-in-law's health, and her own regret that since the death of old Dr. King there had been only his son, a young boy of twenty eight or nine, to minister to the physical ills of Old Chester.

"He can't help being young, I know," said Miss Jane, "but I am sure I hope my sister will not have to consult him this summer. I suppose young doctors must have some patients to practice on, or else they would never get experience, but I don't want him to practice on sister."

Mrs. Dale agreed with her, but in the tone of one who is liberal enough to put up with a necessity. "They've got to be young, some time," she said.

"I suppose so," Jane Temple admitted;

"but really, even I know more about some things, chicken-pox, for instance, than Willie does. When Effie had it, I knew just what to do, and I am sure Willie had to ask his mother before he dared prescribe. And then, in preparing medicine, a young man is apt to be careless. I wish some more experienced person" — Miss Jane's voice was not quite even — "some more experienced person had charge of the drugs."

Mrs. Dale glanced at her over her spectacles, keenly. "Indeed, dear Jane, you are needlessly concerned; Willie is really careful, and beside, his dispensing the medicines is only a temporary arrangement. Tommy Dove is our apothecary usually, and he is old enough, I am sure. He is absent just now, but he is a most capable person. Of course, Old Chester would not encourage any one who was not capable."

Miss Jane bent down to pat Rip's red-brown head. "Yes, he is capable; but—

as you say, he is not here this summer? I noticed, the first time that I went down to the village, that his house was shut up, and all his pretty garden so neglected; it seemed so strange! I — I wondered where — I should say why — I mean where, he had gone?"

She stroked Rip's ears rapidly, the color fluttering into her face.

"Dear me! one would think Jane was interested!" Mrs. Dale said to herself; but aloud she only observed that she was not surprised that her companion thought Mr. Tommy's conduct strange. "In spite of his years, and of the influences about him — though sometimes I think influences amount to very little," said Mrs. Dale, the thought of Ellen heavy upon her heart, — "in spite of everything, Mr. Tommy's conduct shows, I fear, an ill-regulated mind."

"Does it, indeed, ma'am?" Miss Jane asked tremulously. "I always thought him most estimable, — though I have been away so much," she ended weakly.

"Oh," said Mrs. Dale, putting down the little white apron and adjusting her spectacles, "he is, of course, a very estimable person in his walk of life. But, my dear Jane, his leaving Old Chester as he did shows a weak character." She was very grave. "This is really very serious," she thought; "poor foolish girl!"

"I had — I have — a great respect for Mr. Dove," Miss Temple said.

"Every one has," Mrs. Dale agreed, resenting an unspoken reproach. "Indeed, I have sometimes thought I would invite him to tea." Miss Jane drew in her breath, as if something hurt her. "He did the same thing about four years ago," Mrs. Dale went on. "Let me see — why, it was the summer you were here. He disappeared without a word to anybody; such a sensational, foolish thing to do. Don't you remember?"

"I remember," said Miss Jane faintly.

"I heard," Mrs. Dale continued, "that he was in Philadelphia this summer. I don't know what he is doing. But even to see as little of the world as Philadelphia is good for Mr. Tommy."

"Yes."

"No doubt he will come back some time, and then it will be our duty to let him see that we do not approve of him. Still, if he will settle down and marry a — a suitable person you know, no doubt his conduct will be overlooked in time. But I doubt if we can have quite the confidence in him that we had, — eccentricity is more dangerous than mere youth!"

"He must have had good reasons," said Jane Temple; "I am sure he must!" It occurred to her that she was betraying herself, but that did not matter. "I — I knew Mr. Dove quite well, and I — trust his judgment, absolutely," she said, with emphasis, for anger had come to her aid.

"You are too kind, dear Jane," said Mrs. Dale. She was sincerely troubled. "Dear! dear!" she said to herself; "to think that Jane Temple can be so weak!"

Miss Temple's indignation brought a fine glow into her cheek; her eyes shone; she began to feel a warmth about her heart that meant happiness, although she did not know it. She was defending him; how sweet it was to defend him! Never mind if she should not see him again, if he never knew that she "cared." She did care, and that was happiness enough. Mrs. Dale's condescension roused her to sudden self-knowledge. "I have a right to my own life," she thought.

"I think I must go now," she said stiffly. She felt she must be alone to think this thing out, and decide what to do; for, without reasoning about it, she knew she was going to do something to make amends to this man, who had given up his home for her sake. Then, with an effort to seem at ease, she added, "I met Effie, as I came over, and she told me Ellen could not take tea with her to-night; I am so sorry."

The mention of Ellen brought Mrs.

Dale back from her consternation at Jane Temple's folly, to her own troubles. "I am afraid," she said, "that I was a little stern to Euphemia when she came to make her request. I was obliged to send her home somewhat abruptly." And then she explained that Ellen had been naughty, and it was necessary to punish her.

Miss Jane's kind eyes filled with pity. "Dear little Ellen!" she said.

VIII

THE day was long and sad to Mrs. Dale; she was disciplining Ellen according to her light, but she was not hopeful. "She is repenting now," she thought, "but she will have forgotten both her repentance and her naughtiness by to-morrow." As it happened, however, Ellen was too interested in the situation to repent. She had made haste to commit to memory the verses her grandmother had brought her, meditating, as she studied, not upon the sacred words, but upon her wrongs. The verses memorized, she went over to the window and knelt down, her cheek resting on the sill.

She did not want to read any of her

sedate little story-books. The "Parent's Assistant," or "Harry and Lucy," or the Rollo books were not as entertaining as was her own misery. Oh, how long, how long was this cruel punishment to last? For she would never beg Betsey's pardon! Perhaps she should grow old, shut up here in this room. She fancied how, gradually, her clothes would wear out, her hair grow gray, and the dust heap itself about her, as she sat silent, motionless! A moment later she thought that she should not like it, and decided that she would bring her imprisonment to an end: *she would starve herself!* She would not eat any dinner nor any supper. Probably she should die in a few days, and then how sorry everybody would be! She should be going to heaven, so she would not be sorry.

"I'll plume my wings and take my flight,"

said Ellen to herself. But before doing this she would forgive her enemies.

She pictured the scene: Her grandmother would find her lying, white and still, on her bed. She would see that Ellen had eaten nothing; then she would implore her to eat — oh, anything! Yes, fruit-cake if she wished it! But no; Ellen would turn her head away, and whisper that she should rather go to heaven. (The tears were rolling peacefully down her face by this time.) At last her grandmother would say, "Oh, my darling Ellen, I have been very cruel to you; is there anything I can give you for a present?"

Here Ellen stopped crying, and reflected upon what she should accept, to signify her forgiveness. "Yes," she decided to reply, "yes, grandmother, you may give me a wig of long yellow curls, and — a Bible." What a pang that last word would give her grandmother! How it would betray the saintly character to which Mrs. Dale had been so blind! The Bible would not be of much use, as she was going to die immediately. But she might leave it to Effie? "Effie does n't read her Bible as much as I do," Ellen thought, with solemn satisfaction. As for the lovely yellow wig, she would wear that when she was dead. At this thought she wept afresh.

She wondered what would be done with her "things," — her china dishes, her best hat, her little iron bank, into which, on every birthday, her grandmother slipped a gold-piece.

"Why," said Ellen to herself, "I ought to make my will!"

She jumped up at that thought, and began with a blunt, blue lead pencil to inscribe her last wishes upon a large sheet of foolscap. "I leave my geography to Betsey Thomas," she wrote in a round, childish hand, and added, "but she's a cross girl." Here she paused to remember her legatees and her possessions; then, hurriedly, wrote Miss Jane Temple's name, and bit the end of her pencil for two minutes before she could decide what to bequeath to her kind friend. The thought of Miss Jane awoke the remorse for her idolatry, and for a moment that horrible melancholy, which has a physical abiding-place just below the breastbone, dimmed her pleasure in the prospect of death. But to leave Miss Jane a lock of her hair, and Lydia Wright her paper dolls, cheered her to tears; for, with a thrill of pride, she felt her eyes blur with a sudden mist.

This touched her deeply, and she leaned forward, and squeezed her eyes tightly shut, at which one single tear trickled down her cheek and splashed full upon the paper; it made a round blot with a little fringe all about it; she breathed on it to dry it; but as the spot rose into a wet blister, she had a bitter moment of feeling that her heirs might not recognize it as a teardrop. She wondered how it would do to write "*tear*" above it. She wished she could cry some more to make another blot, but alas! interest had dried her eyes, and she could only proceed to divide her property among those who appreciated her so little.

Her horse-hair snakes she bequeathed to Mrs. Temple; "Little Henry and his Bearer" to Mr. Temple.

"I will give my bank to my grandmother," she wrote, but, sighing, added, as older consciences have done before her, "the money in it is for the poor heathen."

She paused here to note with satisfaction the perfection of her teardrop, and to look out over the garden. How hot and bright it was out of doors! There was a bed of scarlet poppies blazing in the sunshine; even the shadows looked hot. She could see, across the lane, the stone posts of Mr. Temple's gate, and that made her think of Effie and of the Bible she must leave her.

Just then she noticed that the telegraph string was jarring and thrilling; that meant that Effie was at the other end of it, and was about to send her a note.

The thought of communication with the outside world made her forget death; she dropped her will, and leaned out of the window. In a moment, slowly and with little jerks, came the bit of folded paper floating over the sunny garden, catching for a perilous instant on the highest twig of the laburnum, and then landing safely among the leaves of the woodbine, below the window. Ellen with trembling fingers unfastened it, and, smoothing the crumpled paper, read: "*Come up to the somer hous after diner.*"

She dropped it dismally. What was the use of Effie's saying that? Why didn't she sympathize?

"*Grandmother won't allow me to go out of my room,*" she wrote. "*She says I must ask Betsey's pardon.*"

She fastened her answer to the line, and watched it flutter back to Effie; but the excitement had faded from her face. "Effie knows grandmother won't let me go up to the summer-house," she said to herself. But Effie's next note explained her meaning.

"*Is the door loked? Can't you get out?*"

"Goodness!" said Ellen. She read it over and over. "The door locked?" Why, no, of course not. And after dinner her grandmother always took a nap — and Betsey Thomas would be carrying in the clothes from the lines on the kitchen green — and there would be no one to see her leave her room! "I won't do it," she said to herself; "only, it would be easy to do it." She was so absorbed and excited that she forgot to send an answer to the note. Very quietly, on tiptoe, she crossed the room, and tried the door. It was not locked; but Ellen stood staring at it with great eyes. This punishment of being obliged to stay in her room she knew well; it had happened only too often before, although never, perhaps, for so serious an offense. But it had never occurred to her that it was voluntary. She went back to the window with a bewildered air, and started to see another note awaiting her among the leaves.

"*Why don't you anser? Are you loked in?*"

Ellen's reply betrayed the agitation of a new idea.

"*I'm not locked in, but I can't get out.*"

She hoped and feared at once that Effie would not send any more notes, but a moment later another little folded temptation came over the string.

"*If you're not loked in, come up to the somer house right after dinner. Your grandmother is wiked to shut you up in prizon. If you beg that servant girl's pardon I'll never speak to you again. Anser if you'll come up to the somer hous.*"

Effie, standing on the locust stump, on the other side of the wall, waited a long time for Ellen's reply; the delay made her first angry, and then scared. Perhaps Mrs. Dale had come in and caught Ellen reading the notes! At this thought she was about to jump down from the stump and run away, when, lo! there was an answer coming slowly along the line. Effie, in her eagerness to get it from the string tore it a little, but she could read it in spite of that: "*I will come.*"

IX

ELLEN had been hurried into decision by hearing Betsey Thomas's careful step upon the stairs, and then the sound of a tray bumping against the door. Betsey must not discover the correspondence, and the only way to prevent that was to consent to Effie's wishes.

With excitement Ellen's appetite had returned, and she was glad to eat the bread and butter and cold meat which had been sent her. The thought of the hot dinner downstairs made this severe diet seem a cruelty which justified rebellion.

As she ate, she was excitedly planning her "escape." Ellen had many a time acted out her own fancies of adventure or peril, but she had never had the chance to make them real, if she chose. Her skill in weaving romance blurred just now the actual fact of her naughtiness and gave the whole situation an unreality and an interest that kept her conscience quiet.

She might as well look over her verses, she thought, until it was time to dismiss this exciting possibility. "He that ruleth his spirit," said Ellen, sitting in the big dimity-covered chair, her hands clasped above her head, and her small heels swinging to and fro, "is greater than he that taketh a city. *Oh!*" — she heard Mrs. Dale's step upon the stairs; then the closing of her bedroom door.

Ellen, sat with parted lips; the clock in the lower hall struck three. The great moment had come! She rose stealthily, and, opening her door, looked out into the hall. Then a sudden gush of determination took the little temptation she had played with and carried it into action. She was bewildered, absorbed, fascinated, to find herself yielding — yielding! She had not supposed she was really going to do it; her own possibility intoxicated her; hardly breathing, she slipped on tiptoe out of the room, past her grandmother's door, and then, step by step, downstairs.

It was a still August day. Far off, beyond the meadows at the foot of the terrace, came, through the thinning leaves, the sparkle and flash of the river; nearer, in the stone vase in the middle of the garden, a bunch of scarlet geraniums blazed and glowed. Rip lay stretched on the warm dust of the carriage road at the foot of the steps. There was a scent of hot sunshine in the hazy air. Ellen, palpitating with excitment, stood a moment on the porch, and looked at it all, then she heard a step somewhere in the silent house and darted like a bird out into the freedom of the sunshine! Three minutes later she had reached the summer-house, and Effie, awaiting her for half an hour, was crying out for particulars.

"Wait till I — get — my — breath " — Ellen gasped. When she did get her breath, they talked in whispers, though there was no one nearer than Betsey taking the clothes off the lines down on the kitchen green; but considering, how astonished Betsey would have been could she have overheard that conversation, it was no wonder that they whispered.

Suddenly Ellen jumped up. "Oh, Effie, what time do you think it is? Oh, I'm afraid it's late!"

"No, it is n't," Effie reassured her; "only, may be you'd better go. Now don't forget: if she does n't apologize to you, you are to be here to-morrow morning, with some clothes and food and your bank; and I'll be here with my things, and " —

"Oh, Effie, I *must* run! Grandmother will be downstairs, and then what shall I do? Oh, Effie, I must go!" Ellen stamped her foot with impatient fright.

But Mrs. Dale had not yet come downstairs from her nap, so Ellen was able to regain her room quite unobserved. There, with a wildly beating heart, she opened her Bible for a look at the verses; the habit of doing as she was bid made this final study instinctive, but she could hardly see the words, much less feel their meaning.

"I will certainly do it," she assured herself; "and oh, what will Lydia say? Yes, I will not come back until I am twenty years old. By that time grandmother will know that she can't order me around, and starve me, and treat me so cruelly; and very likely Betsey Thomas will be married then — in nine years."

The two children had arranged how they were to support themselves during these years of absence, in which their families were to repent. "We'll go to a city," Effie had said vaguely. And once there, they were to be milliners. There had been a moment's wavering in favor of a candy-shop, but reflection upon the amount of money Mrs. Temple paid for her bonnets decided them, for, as Ellen pointed out, if they sold a dozen **twenty**-five-dollar bonnets a day, they could well afford to buy candy, instead of serving behind a counter for the chance to eat it. Effie explained incidentally that her reason for including herself in these delightful plans was that her aunt Jane made her life a burden, and tried all the time to make Mrs. Temple "cross."

Everything being thus arranged, it only remained for Ellen to have firmness in the coming interview with her grandmother. It occurred to the child to consider as an interesting possibility, what she should do if her grandmother were to have a change of heart before the carefully planned retribution could fall upon her. Suppose Mrs. Dale should say she were sorry? It would be disappointing, but such things had been, and it was well to be prepared. Suppose she were to say, "Ellen, I was very unkind, and Betsey Thomas shall beg your pardon. And what would you like me to do for you?"

Ellen put her cheek down on the open Bible and meditated. She would like to have all the pin-wheels and fire-crackers that she wanted; also torpedoes, — those little white bags of flame and noise; with these she would give an exhibition to the village, especially to the tannery hands. The thought of her own importance and beneficence, in thus officiating, filled her with a glow of self-approval which seemed to fade into a blur of general satisfaction, and the next thing she knew, she heard Betsey Thomas saying, "Waken up, Ellen; your grandmother is waiting down on the porch to hear you say your verses. Wake up, and let me brush your hair and tidy you up a bit."

Betsey was very much affected by observing that Ellen had fallen asleep upon the open page of her Bible, and she made haste to report it to Mrs. Dale, who was likewise somewhat impressed by it. It made her ready to forgive the child at once, and to hope that Ellen had been seeking a higher forgiveness.

Ellen gathered up her courage, and went slowly downstairs; and then, in her fresh white apron, her brown hair tucked smoothly behind her little ears, and her hands folded in front of her, she stood before Mrs. Dale, and repeated quite perfectly the half dozen verses she had been told to learn. With downcast eyes she listened in dutiful silence to her grandmother's admonitions. "And now, Ellen," Mrs. Dale said, with a sigh of relief that this trying day was ended, — "now, Ellen, I hope that you will always remember your duty as a little Christian child, and never forget that a lady is as courteous to those whom God has placed in a different station as to her own friends. You may kiss me goodnight, my child, and then go and tell Betsey Thomas that you are sorry. To-morrow morning you will turn over a new leaf and start out fresh."

Ellen was quite pale. "No 'm," she said briefly.

"You mean it shall never happen again? I am very glad, my dear. And I am sure you have asked your Heavenly Father to forgive you, also?"

Ellen's response of silence to appeals of this kind always confused Mrs. Dale; like one who pronounces a magic formula and sees no result, she was vaguely disturbed. It had happened many, many times, but she never grew accustomed to the pain of it. "Now go to Betsey Thomas," she said, with the sternness which means embarrassment.

"No 'm," Ellen said. "I don't want to, grandmother."

In the explanation which followed this, and in the order that she was to go to bed without any supper, and spend the next day, until she apologized to Betsey, in her own room, it seemed to the child as though she could hear her heart beat. It did not occur to Mrs. Dale, grieved and anxious, and viewing the situation with a seriousness of which it was not worthy, that some patient reasoning might have brought the suggestion of apology from the child's own lips, although she would have been the first to realize that such an impulse from within would have counted more in character than when it was the result of insistence from without.

Perhaps the whole difficulty was in Mrs. Dale's lack of imagination; but, besides that, it must be admitted that it is not easy for a righteous and inflexible will to concede a point. Indeed, it would be interesting to know how much the sense of personal dignity is responsible for mistakes made in the training of children; mistakes which apparently do not injure the children very much, — for, after all, we most of us turn out pretty well, — but from which the characters of the elders certainly suffer.

X

MISS JANE TEMPLE was strangely distrait that afternoon. She forgot her sister-in-law's beef tea at four, and glass of sherry at six. She told Effie, briefly, that she would not play backgammon with her after tea. "I have — some writing to do," she explained, in answer to the child's impatient protest, and there was something in her voice that made Mrs. Temple look up and say, —

"Is there anything the matter, Janey?"

"Oh, no, dear sister," she answered. "Come, Effie; I'll play just one game; but I really am too busy to play any more than that."

Effie ran for the board, but she was as

nervous as her aunt, and the single game was more than enough for her. Her impatience worried her mother, so that she was sent to bed, stamping her foot as she went, to Mrs. Temple's further annoyance.

"I don't know why Effie is n't like that dear little Ellen," said Mrs. Temple, with a sigh. "Now she has gone, Janey, write down here, won't you? Who are you going to write to?"

Miss Jane's face flushed suddenly and painfully. "I — well — I have to write to a — friend," she stammered.

Mrs. Temple raised herself on her elbow, and looked at her with undisguised curiosity. "Why, Janey, one would think you were a girl writing to her lover."

Miss Jane's laugh was so forced and conscious that Mrs. Temple was fairly breathless with astonishment. "Why, Jane Temple!" she said. But the younger woman had hurried upstairs for her writing materials. Mrs. Temple fell back among her cushions with a puzzled face.

"Why," she said to herself, "what does it mean? Who can she be writing to? That Dove man? Is it possible?"

But when her sister-in-law came back with her little old rosewood writing-desk, which folded over on itself, and was lined with faded purple velvet, Mrs. Temple was quite apologetic. "I did n't mean to seem curious, Janey; I did not know that you had any secrets of that kind. I'm sure I beg your pardon?" She could not help the question in her voice, nor an injured look.

"Of course, dear Euphemia, I know that. I — I only just have a letter — of no importance, to write. I thought I would write it to-night, though."

"It *is* to Mr. Dove," said Mrs. Temple to herself. "Dear me! I would not have thought that of Janey! Still, I don't know why she should n't be friendly to the poor little man; he would never dare to presume upon it. And Janey never would leave us." Mrs. Temple grew tearful at the thought, but Miss Jane was too absorbed in the composition of a very brief letter to notice the invalid. That love develops selfishness is readily granted by those who are not lovers.

Miss Temple wrote a line, and paused; then she made some straight marks on her blotting-paper, and looked at them thoughtfully; after that, she mended her pen, and took a fresh sheet, and began her letter again; but stopped a moment to press down the curling corners of the worn velvet lining of her desk.

"You don't write very much," Mrs. Temple observed, with something like malice in her voice; and certainly, in a half hour, it was not unreasonable to suppose that more than half a page should be written.

"There is my stamp box, Janey, dear," she ventured, a little later, and Miss Jane thanked her, but said she had stamped her envelope.

"So it is n't to anybody in Old Chester," Mrs. Temple assured herself. "Yes, it must be to Mr. Tommy!" Mrs. Temple was growing interested and amiable.

"I'm sure I don't want to seem to pry," she said, with a little cough behind her thin white hand, as; with a quickened breath, Miss Jane suddenly put down her pen, and folded her letter; "I don't want to pry, but it seems to me that a letter that puzzles one to write, as that has evidently puzzled you, should be — well, I should think you would want advice. Not that I want to give advice. I should be quite unwilling to advise; only I'd — give it a good deal of thought, if I were you," she ended weakly.

"I have," answered Miss Temple gently. Then the determination with which she had folded the letter seemed to desert her, and for a moment she held it with tremulous hesitation. "I have thought," she repeated, absently. And then she seemed to come to herself and remember her duties. "Are n't you ready now for your gruel, dear sister?" she said. "I'll go and get it." She put the letter in her pocket and rose.

Mrs. Temple shut her eyes and whimpered, "I'm sure I didn't mean to be impertinent. You're very unkind to me, Janey."

Miss Jane was full of protestations; "Why! of course nothing you could say would be impertinent. Indeed, I'm always grateful for your interest. Now, won't you sit up and take this gruel?" Her voice was nervous with unspoken excuses.

She slipped her arm under the invalid's head and held the bowl to her lips, and said she was sure Mrs. Temple was a little stronger, and she did think that gray silk wrapper was so becoming.

But she did not mention the address of the letter.

XI

THE next morning Ellen was awake and staring, wide-eyed, at the dawn, long before the maids, in the faint light, went yawning down to the kitchen.

It seemed, when she awoke, as though some terrible dream had oppressed her, and she felt for a moment that sense of wondering relief, which grown persons know too well, and that fades so instantly into miserable certainty. Ellen, with a frightened sigh, remembered; and then buried her face in her pillow, and felt the tears behind her eyes, though no tears came. Older persons know this pain, too. For relief, the child began to think of what she had promised to do.

It was impossible! How had she ever dared to think of such a thing? Yet how could she break her promise to Effie? The honesty of that thought drove her into planning the details of this impossible action. She must make her arrangements, even though she might not be able to carry them out. First she must pack her "things" up in something. She began to think of a certain leather bag which had belonged to her grandfather; she saw it in her memory, — the sole leather worn and shabby, and the "Eben Dale" in fat black letters on one side. She must get that bag. She must — *steal it!* Well, she had nothing else, she couldn't help it; it wasn't her fault; she had to have a bag; poor little Ellen! She was knowing the confusion of older sinners: self-blame and self-pity.

The bag was in the spare room across the hall. She was afraid of this rarely used room, it was so dark and silent, and once her grandfather had lain dead in it!

No one guessed what terrors had shaken the child whenever she had had to enter it. She used to run past its closed door, flinging a scared look over her shoulder; it seemed to her that some time the door would open, and *something* stand on the threshold; she never said what would stand there, her terror needed no detail of words. Oh, how hard it was that the bag should be in that room!

She crept out of bed, and without waiting to dress stole across the hall and softly pushed the spare room door open; the shutters were bowed, and one thin line of the sweet morning light came in from the dawn outside, touching, like a pointing finger, the great bed, draped in its white valance and coverlet. Its four mahogany posts made Ellen think of the obelisk which marked Dr. Dale's grave in the churchyard. The noiseless, lifting line of the sunbeam lay upon the white matting, almost at her feet; she stopped, then stepped across it, with a gasp. After that, though the tide of resolution rose and fell, the deed was practically done; in the child's mind arose confusedly the vision of the sword of tremulous flame outside the gate of Paradise. The morning sunbeam and the little child made the picture of a human heart's profanity. Ellen felt, but did not understand, this critical moment created by her imagination.

Suddenly she thought the valance about the bed fluttered, and she almost cried out, and then stood with staring eyes. Oh, what if there were something under that awful bed? There was a moment of strained silence; then, on tiptoe, looking sideways at the valance, she glided across the room; never once did she turn her back upon the bed; it seemed as though, if she glanced away for an instant, she should see, when she looked back, the long straight lines of the sheet, as she had seen them three years before. When at last she held the bag in her hand, and crept towards the door, a glimpse of herself in the glass, in her white night-gown, with wide, terrified eyes, startled her so that she almost dropped it.

When the first fright was over, Ellen began to pack her dearly bought valise. How silent the house was! The wet leaves of the woodbine outside her window began to shine as the sun looked around the corner of the house; some birds twittered; she heard a latch lift and fall, and knew that the women were going downstairs. It was very exciting. She must hurry with her packing, she thought, or Betsey Thomas might discover her.

What should she take with her? Her best dress, certainly; but she found, on squeezing it into the smallest possible bundle, that there would be little room for anything else in the bag, and drew it out again, meshed with wrinkles. In its place she put a small china vase, and then sat down upon the floor to reflect upon what else was necessary. Her Sunday hat, of course. The soft leghorn, with its white ribbons, was easily rolled up and pushed into the yawning jaws of the bag. Boots, — she should need boots? "I might get my feet wet," she considered, proud to find how practical she was. So, hastily, she dropped a pair of shoes in beside the hat; and then, with a quick impulse, tucked her Bible in one corner. This gave her tortured little conscience a momentary relief; it was so good to take her Bible! Her bank? She had almost forgotten her bank. That would have been, indeed, a serious omission. And here she came to an end of her packing; there was really nothing else to take; money, boots, a hat, and a Bible, — what else was needed for a journey? So she pushed the bag under the bed, that it might escape Betsey's eyes when she should enter with the tray and breakfast. But Betsey, when she came, did not glance about the room, nor speak to Ellen; following Mrs. Dale's directions, she put the tray down, silently, and went away.

Ellen debated within herself whether she should eat her breakfast or put it in her bag. She decided on the former course, for, as the food was to be eaten some time, as well now as later. Breakfast over, came the waiting until nine o'clock, when she was to escape by means of the back stairs. She was greatly excited, and when, suddenly, her bedroom door opened, she started so violently that Betsey Thomas tried to reassure her, before delivering a message from Mrs. Dale.

"Don't be scared, Ellen; law, it's only me. And Ellen, why don't you be a good girl? I don't mind nothin'! You just say you'll apologize, child. Do, now, Ellen," she said anxiously.

Ellen did not answer. "Anyway, your grandmother says you are to go out of doors for an hour and walk; and then she says — well, says she, 'Ellen can come and see me, *if she's anything to say!*' Do, Ellen. I wish 't you would, child?"

Ellen looked out of the window to hide

the tears that were trembling on her lashes.

"Your grandmother has a headache, she ain't up yet," Betsey ended significantly, her hand upon the door-knob; and then she turned back to add, "I'm to leave your dinner on the chest of drawers in the back entry, Ellen, and you're to get it yourself, your grandmother says."

The little girl looked scared; had she made her grandmother ill? She had promised Effie,—she must not break her word; but how dreadful if she had made her grandmother ill! Oh, how unhappy she was! She kept saying over and over to herself that she had "promised Effie;" and so she must go. But when, with her bag in her hand, she started, ostensibly for the hour's walk in the garden, it was still incredible to her that she should be able to keep her word. She stopped a moment in the upper hall to wipe her eyes, and then, feeling very homesick, she crept to her grandmother's door, and, kneeling down, kissed the knob, softly.

There was no sound behind the closed door, for Mrs. Dale had had her coffee and dropped into a nap; but the lack of any response to her burst of affection made Ellen's old bitterness come back; the sense of being badly treated put her mind again into the comfortable grooves of habit, and an unreal wretchedness made her so much happier, that she was able to be interested in the situation, and say to herself that she was "escaping!" She actually sauntered through the gooseberry bushes of the kitchen garden, taking the exercise which her grandmother had permitted her. The lawful prelude to an unlawful event had its charm for Ellen.

She said to herself that her absence would not be discovered until the afternoon, for Betsey Thomas would not go for the tray before three o'clock, at the earliest.

Effie was waiting for her on the summer-house steps, looking quite pale. Before Ellen reached her she began to talk in an agitated way. "Ellen, do you know, I believe — I — I *can't*. I'm not going to. I'm awfully sorry — but — aunty wants me to have a dress fitted this afternoon. And, don't you see, I can't? I'm awfully sorry." Effie was very much embarrassed.

Ellen was out of breath; the bag, with all that money in the iron bank, was heavy. She stopped, and put it down on the step, and looked up at Effie silently. Effie was very nervous.

"Well, you see, I can't help it; I've got to have my dress fitted. It is n't my fault. And *you* can do it just the same."

"Do you mean," said Ellen in a low voice, "that you've backed out?"

Effie began to cry. "Well, what's the use? I'm not like you; my papa's not dead, and he'd catch me right off. Besides, he's awfully fond of me. So what's the use?"

"All right."

"Oh, Nellie, you're not mad? You can go, all the same. I've brought you lots of food to take. Only you must n't tell that I did; they 'd scold me."

"Of course I shall go all the same. If you don't tell, you won't be scolded."

"Oh, I won't tell," Effie promised with a gasp; "only, don't you think they might find out? They 'll think I ought to have told on you."

Ellen's lip quivered. "I guess they won't find out," she said; "but I did n't suppose it was right to break your word, Effie Temple."

"Oh, well, if you are going to get mad," said Effie, "I would n't go for anything! I hate people that get mad."

Ellen swallowed hard, and, turning away from Effie, blinked several times.

"What have you got in your bag?" Effie began, softening a little. "Any cake? And, Nellie, I thought I 'd just say, '*I don't think you ought to go.*' Now, I 'm not to blame; so let 's plan. See the things I brought: eggs — they are not boiled — and cake. Look! is n't that nice?"

"I don't want your cake," said Ellen, her little red lower lip quivering, "and I don't want to make any more plans with you. I'm going now; good-by, Euphemia Temple. I'll never speak to you again."

Effie was divided between interest and anger, in which there was also a little fear that Ellen would not go, and so all this excitement would come to an end. "It's real mean to talk that way just because I can't go. I have awfully pretty dresses, not like yours; and they have to be fitted. I won't tell — and — don't you, either, when you come back. I mean, if you come back. And write to me, Nellie. Oh, my goodness, I wish I was going. Gracious! it's splendid!"

Such admiration touched Ellen, who had already reached the lower step. "Yes, I'll write to you," she said, "though I don't think you are a very good friend." It did not occur to Ellen that here was her opportunity to "back out." Somehow, this deflection only strengthened her purpose; very likely, had Effie been faithful, and urged her, she would have had some wholesome hesitation.

Effie stood up, shading her eyes with her hand, and watching Ellen's little figure flit across the orchard and down the hill to the highway. There, the elderberry bushes that fringed the road hid her for a moment, and then she was swallowed up in a cloud of dust, as a wagon went jogging by.

So began Ellen's journey into the world.

XII

THE sun poured hot and white upon the long stretch of sandy road. Ellen had hurried through the village, and, as it chanced, met no one. Near the post-office, on the main street, she saw a familiar figure which gave her an instant's fear. It was Miss Jane Temple; she had a letter in her hand, and seemed to be reading its address, with absent intentness; she never once looked up. Escaped from those friendly eyes, Ellen was soon beyond Old Chester.

She walked steadily, and quite rapidly; she passed two or three people; one man, who knew her, said, "Hullo, Ellen!" in a surprised way, but asked no questions.

After that she walked for a while in the fields along the road, so that she might not be seen. The bag was heavy, and so was her heart.

It was nearly dinner time. She had rejected Effie's cake and eggs, and those friendly berries, which in story-books offer themselves to wandering children, did not appear. There were locust-trees here and there by the roadside, but they had nothing to give her but a flickering shade. She really wished very much that she had eaten more breakfast. If she could see a shop, she would open her bank, she thought, and buy something. But not only were there no shops in sight; there were no houses, either.

She had taken every cross-road and lane and turn, and walked through fields, and skirted meadows, and now had quite lost her bearings, and had no idea where she was. The reaching the railroad at Mercer seemed simple enough when she and Effie talked it over, but where was

Mercer? She stumbled a little as she plodded through the dust, and then said to herself that she was so tired she must sit down and rest.

It was just noon. The mowed fields on either side of the road lay in a hot blur of sunshine; the long z-z-ing of the locusts seemed to emphasize the stillness. So far, the child had been sustained by excitement, and anger at Effie, and consciousness of achievement; but little by little a dull ache of reality was beginning to make itself felt. She perceived, far off, the moment when resolution would flag. But it was very far off. She would still pretend to herself that she was going to Mercer. Down the white road a little cloud of dust was creeping along; Ellen could hear a slow creaking jolt before she could distinguish in the dusty nimbus a peddler's cart. It was covered with sunburned canvas, and as all the weight was on the front seat, it tilted up behind and sagged upon the front wheels. The white mule which jogged between the shafts was driven by a large person with a ruddy face; he wore spectacles, whose round silver rims looked like little satellites of his moon-like countenance, which had also a halo about it, made by a fringe of white whiskers under his chin, and a gray felt hat, worn on the back of his head. His elbows were on his knees, and the reins hung loosely between his fingers; he was humming to himself, and once or twice his head nodded, as though he were half asleep; indeed, his eyes were closed, and he would not have noticed Ellen, standing at the roadside, had not the mule come to a standstill to kick a fly from its gray, shaggy stomach.

"Hallo!" said the man, opening his eyes.

"Yes, sir," said Ellen nervously.

"Warm day."

"Yes, sir."

"Goin' my way?"

"Yes, sir," Ellen said, having not the slightest idea where he was going.

"Edward and me'll give thee a lift; git in."

"Oh, no, thank you, sir, I — I'm going to Mercer." Her voice quivered, so that the peddler looked at her with sudden scrutiny. "Hallo, what's this?" said he.

"Why, sissy, Mercer is twenty miles off! Come, thee'd better git in; I'm goin' that way."

There was something so pleasant in the kindliness of his face that Ellen, tired, and afraid of her own thoughts, and dumbfounded at the idea of the twenty miles still before her, found herself saying, "Thank you, sir," and climbing in over the wheel.

The white mule pricked up first one ear and then the other, and with reluctance began to move; his master turned his friendly spectacles upon Ellen. "Thee's a little tot to be going to Mercer by theeself," he said.

Ellen did not reply.

There was a pause, in which the peddler

seemed to seek a meaning in her silence, and then he said, with clumsy and painstaking gentleness, "Does th' folks know thee's going to Mercer, sissy?"

"I think I'll get out and walk," Ellen said agitatedly. The peddler made a little clucking sound, as though to soothe her; and then he chuckled to himself, but did not stop Edward; he only said, "Here's a joke!" Ellen politely tried to call up a smile, but she saw nothing funny. She wished she had not gotten into the cart.

"I'm going to be a milliner," she said, with childish embarrassment at silence.

"Well, now, ain't that strange? I'm in the millinery way, myself; though I'm a literary man. I sell books. There's nothin' like literature for improvin' folks." He paused, and beamed upon Ellen. "Like books?"

"Yes, sir, I like to read very much," she answered. Ellen was vain of this liking to read. She had often heard Betsey Thomas speak of it with admiration and wonder.

The peddler nodded his head; his spectacles had a kindly gleam in them. "I can't say that I'm particular about readin' books, but I like 'em. And I like to sell 'em. My house is full of 'em. Thee's welcome to look at 'em."

"Thank you, sir, but I think I mustn't stop," returned Ellen, feeling snubbed, for this gentleman was evidently contemptuous about reading. "I am going on to Mercer."

"Thee has no call to stop," the man explained. "This is my house, this cart. I sleep in it, and eat in it, and follow my literary pursuits in it. A-puttin' th' house on wheels don't stop its bein' th' house, huh?"

"Oh, no, sir," Ellen assured him nervously.

"Yes; look around, look around and make theeself at home. This here seat we're settin' on is the front piazza; that there shelf, back, is my bedroom; this here roomy space, right behind us, is the parlor; and right behind it — see that chalk line?" (he had fastened the reins on a hook in the wagon frame above his head, so that he could turn and direct Ellen's glances about the cart) — "that chalk line is the wall between the kitchen and parlor. When it rains I go in off the piazza and set in my parlor, and Edward, he goes on. Them boxes on the shelf overhead is my garret; they're full of finery — ribbons and such things. The ladies will have them. Now, for me, I'd rather have books. There's the library under my bed. All convenient, all right to th' hand. Honest, I pities the people with them big, uneasy houses. So lonesome in 'em, they must be!"

Ellen was much interested; she began to think that she would go about in a cart, instead of being a milliner. Perhaps she'd better ask this kind gentleman's advice as to where she could get a cart, and a white mule like Edward? (But all the while, in the background of her heart, she saw herself at home again.)

She could not ask her question at once, because the peddler stopped at the door of a farmhouse; and Ellen, curled up on the seat, watched the ingratiating politeness with which he enticed a reluctant customer. He looked over his glasses, nodding his head in candid assent to each objection that was made, as though he had no personal interest in disposing of his goods. He showed a beguiling sympathy for the purchaser's economical hesitation, a sympathy which was almost an entreaty not to purchase, and that could not but result in a sale. When they drove away, followed by a barking dog, and leaving a yard of cotton lace in exchange for the money jingling in the peddler's hand, he began to sing to himself; he seemed to have forgotten Ellen, who felt neglected.

"I think perhaps I'd like to sell things in a cart," she said, with some dignity and resentment.

Her host interrupted his singing, and looked at her. Then he chuckled. "It's a good business. Course it's some lonesome. Thee might be dyin' in th' house, lyin' there in the parlor, fer instance, and not one 'ud care; but thee's free, in this business; thee's shut of all th' friends that boss thee — and want th' money!" said the peddler, with a sudden seriousness of his own.

"I think it would be very pleasant to play house in a wagon," said Ellen, struggling against the depression of possible loneliness, and a little disappointed that no reference was made to the sorrow of deserted friends.

"Yes; yes, 't is," the peddler admitted. "But nights, now, fer instance. Lyin' there in thy bedroom, hoo! thee don't know what 'll come at thee in the dark!"

Ellen was instantly frightened. "I — I think I won't," she said faintly. "I guess I'll be a milliner."

"Well, that's genteel; and yet they do say that they starve, the milliners, mostly. Graveyards is full of 'em."

"Why, but," Ellen protested, "bonnets are twenty-five dollars apiece; I should think they 'd be rich, the milliners?"

Among the peddler's customers, ladies who paid twenty-five dollars for a bonnet were not frequent, but he wisely avoided the discussion. Instead, he remarked, "Yes, and fifty dollars! But thee sees, the fifties and the twenty-fives comes to gentlemen in my line. The milliners have to get their things from us. They don't make much."

This was beyond Ellen, but, though she did not understand it, it left her in doleful uncertainty in regard to her plans. She sighed, and turned the subject by asking the peddler if he ever thought that maybe he was dreaming.

"Huh?" said the man, slapping a rein on Edward's back, and turning the puzzled benevolence of his mild eyes upon her.

But Ellen found it hard to explain. This thought of the possible unreality of the present had always been a vague terror, for it usually haunted her happiest moments. Suppose it was all a dream, — her pleasant life, her paper dolls, her little teas with Lydia, her garden, and the swing under the front porch, — a dream, and she really a poor little beggar, about to awake to hunger and cold and misery? But now, when she put the question to the peddler, she thought how happy she would be if she awoke and found *this* a dream!

"I only meant," she said, trying to keep her voice from trembling, "that I don't know how we know we're not dreaming. Sometimes I think I'll waken up and find I'm — a Laplander, all dressed up in skins, and milking reindeers, and living in a tent; or" — Ellen began to get interested, in spite of the ache in her heart that made talking an effort — "or, maybe, a Chinese baby, in a cradle all painted with dragons, and my feet squeezed up."

"Well, I swan!" said the peddler. He looked at Ellen, curiously; it occurred to him that she was crazy.

"Don't you ever think those things?" she asked eagerly.

"Well, now thee 's said it, — I *don't*," the man admitted gravely. "Poor little tot!" he said to himself, "she ain't just right, I guess."

"Oh, I think about it lots," Ellen assured him. "Sometimes I think" — this in a lowered voice, for it was a very secret thought, with which she comforted herself when Betsey Thomas was more than usually aggravating, and which she had never confided even to Lydia — "I think I 'm the queen's daughter, and when I wake I 'll be in a golden palace. And then, other times, I 've thought that it was n't a dream, but only that it was a secret from me, and people did n't want me to know I was a queen's daughter, yet. They wanted me to be brought up in a republican country, you know. But I 'll be sent for when I 'm eighteen, and all the prime ministers and grand viziers and congressmen will come, and kneel down, and say, 'You 're a princess, and here's your crown!'" Ellen's face had cleared, as if some morning wind had blown away the clouds of a spring dawn. "Just think!" she cried; "wouldn't it be splendid! My!"

"Well, well," said the peddler, "I guess th' folks don't find the handlin' of thee real easy? There, now, sissy, it ain't healthy to have them dreams. Didn't thy ma ever tell thee so?"

"My mother's gone to heaven, and so has my father," said Ellen. "I live with grandmother." She turned her head away with a confused look. The fact that she was an orphan was not at all a grief to Ellen, for she did not remember her parents, but it was an embarrassment; it meant that she needed the prayers of the Church, and the clause "protect and provide for all fatherless children" made her, every Sunday, turn hot and red at the publicity of her condition. She was relieved when the peddler requested Edward to stop, and observed that it was time for dinner.

She brightened, and immediately felt that life was real. It was after three, and she was positively faint with hunger. They drew up on the shady side of the road, and she watched the peddler hang a battered canvas bag full of oats about Edward's neck; then he went around to the back of the wagon to reach his kitchen.

"I'm goin' to cook my dinner," he said. His spectacles had such a friendly gleam that Ellen felt happier, in spite of that weight upon her heart. But the moment of return seemed very near!

"There's an open place back in there, under the trees, nice and grassy; I call it the restaurant. I always cook there when I go by this way. There's a spring, too. Edward, he stays by, to mind the cart."

He lifted out a queer little stove, and then a frying-pan and a sauce-pan, and a basket in which seemed to be various articles of food. "May be thee'd like to look at a book for a while," he said, "until thee gits th' own dinner?"

He handed Ellen a pamphlet bound in yellow paper, and then pushed the bushes aside and disappeared into the woods. Ellen looked listlessly at the cover of the book, on which was a print of a lady in blue, with feathers in her hair, and a gentleman in red, with a sword; she was wondering how soon the dinner would be cooked. The peddler did not come back. There was only Edward, flinging up his head occasionally and crunching his oats, to keep her company. The wagon had been drawn up close to the roadside, so that other vehicles might pass, but there were none in sight; the woods on either side were thick and still; a rod away a thread of water fell with a musical sound from a hollowed log into a rusty iron caldron. Edward glanced at it patiently once or twice. It made Ellen thirsty, the faint gleam and drip and bubbling sound, but she dared not leave the cart to get a drink, lest the peddler might return to say that dinner was ready.

As she sat there a savory smell of cooking came through the bushes; it was really very hard to wait so long. She tried to forget her hunger by reading the little book. It was the story in rhyme of Lord Belchan and Lady Susey Pye. The pictures were rough prints, in the primary colors, of lords and ladies, parrots and castles, strange ships and battles. "Lord Belchan," she read —

> "Lord Belchan was a noble lord,
> A noble lord of high degree,
> And he determinèd to go abroad,
> Strange countries for to see!"

But Ellen was too hungry to be interested. She began to wonder whether the peddler had forgotten her. At last she could bear it no longer, and, climbing down from the cart, she went timidly into the woods. It was so dark and shadowy under the trees, that for an instant she did not see the peddler, sitting, his arms clasped about his knees, gazing anxiously in her direction. A look of relief came into his face, followed by an affectation of vast indifference.

"Well, sissy," he said, "has thee had th' dinner?"

"My dinner!" Ellen faltered. "Why — I"— She stood quite still, looking at him, her little chin quivering — and her eyes filling. It was more than those kindly spectacles could stand. "There, now; well, well; come, child, eat a bit, here. I don't mind givin' thee a little; though it ain't what's done in the world. It's everybody fer themselves — when a lady or gentleman don't have no use fer friends, and has left 'em! Course, thee knows it ain't nothin' to me ef thee's hungry. I only look out for myself." He turned his back upon the child, for he could not bear those slow, rolling tears, and he heaped a tin plate with a queer combination of fried meat and potatoes. "Eat that," he said gruffly; and then, with instant softening, "There, now, sissy! But 't ain't like home: I was just pointin' that out to thee, that's all."

Ellen silently took the tin plate and began to eat.

"Of course," the peddler said, "of course thee mustn't expect, after this, folks thee's got no claim on will feed thee, now thee's got shut of th' friends. Thee knows the Good Book allows that if a man don't do his own peddling, he ain't to eat. But thee's free, and of course it's fine to be free."

"I have my bank, sir, and I'll pay you for my dinner," said Ellen, a trembling dignity in her voice; "and I guess I'll go now."

"Go?" said the peddler; "thee means to Mercer? Well, Edward an' I'll be joggin' on soon, and we'll take thee."

Ellen did not answer. Oh, how could she get away from this dreadful man, who was dragging her to Mercer? The friendly feeling that had accompanied her confidences, faded; "I *won't* go to Mercer!" she thought; and experienced the relief of being angry at somebody else for her own wrong-doing, a relief often sought by sinners of more advanced years.

The peddler had gone out into the road to water Edward, but came back again and sat down on the soft forest grass between the roots of a great chestnut. "We'll rest a bit on Edward's account," he said, "and then we'll go on. I believe I'll just shut my eyes for about five minutes."

He stretched himself out on the ground, and, putting the felt hat over his eyes, crossed his hands upon his breast. He was chuckling to himself over this adventure with a runaway child, and planning, with an imagination as fertile as Ellen's own, the delight of her family when he should return her, safe and sound, which he meant to do about six o'clock. "I can't shunt off no customer fer the little tot," he reflected, "but I'll get her home by six. I guess her grandma'll be a good customer after this."

The cooking-stove stood in the little plot of forest grass, with the untidy tin plates resting on its cooling top; a spring, bubbling up between some flat stones, chattered to itself; a bird piped in the tree overhead, and then came fluttering down into the open space. It looked with bright, quick eyes at Ellen, sitting in her miserable heart-sick silence, and then hopped across the little glade, where the shadows lay like a lattice upon moss and grass, and began to peck at the scraps of food on the plates. Through the bushes Ellen could see Edward's ears twitching now and then, and the rusty canvas of the cart. Into the wood quiet came the sharp sound of trotting hoofs, and then an instant's glimpse of a man on horseback. It brought her heart up into her throat; he came, whoever he was, from that world which she had left. Oh, if she could catch him, — if she could make him take her home!

The inevitable moment had come.

The peddler slept tranquilly. Silently, like a little thief, Ellen rose, and stepped stealthily across the grass. The bird, startled, dashed up into the greenery overhead, but the peddler never stirred. As she gained the road, Edward, standing with patient bowed head, cocked one gray ear at the rustle of the leaves, but, not seeing his master, drowsed again.

Ellen, terrified lest she might hear a step crashing through the underbrush behind her, fled like a hare down the road in the direction in which the man on horseback had gone; she would catch him, she said to herself, and then beg him to take her home. She ran, poor child, until it seemed as though the beating in her throat would suffocate her; and then, exhausted, she fell down on the grass beside the road. She had run, of course, a very short distance, but she thought that she had covered miles. As soon as she could get her breath, she remembered that if she stopped, the peddler, assisted by Edward, would quickly overtake her. And yet she could not run any farther. If she crept behind the bushes at the roadside, he surely could not see her, should he pass? So she pushed through some underbrush, climbed a fence, and reached a wide meadow. There, lying down on the grass near some bushes, she said to herself that she would rest a little while, and then start again for home.

XIII

THE child was so tired that scarcely had her head touched the grass than she fell fast asleep, — too soundly to hear the peddler calling her, anxiously, his voice pathetic with mortification that he had let her slip away from him; too soundly, also, even to dream of the dismay and anxiety in the home she had left.

Mrs. Dale's headache, which had kept her awake nearly all night, yielded after she had had her coffee and sent her message to Ellen, and faded into an exhausted slumber which lasted until noon. Betsey Thomas, who at first was full of pity for the naughty child, began to resent her obstinacy, fearing that presently she herself would be blamed for a *contretemps* which would not have come about save for her well-meant interference. This half-frightened resentment made her keep to herself the fact that Ellen's dinner-tray had not been touched. "I ain't a-goin' to be blamed if Ellen sets up to be obstinate about her victuals," she said to herself sulkily. But a little later, when she caught a glimpse of Effie Temple wandering about in the orchard, her sense of justice, to say nothing of her desire to excuse herself, made her say to the cook that she "had a mind to tell Mrs. Dale that that hateful little girl put our Ellen up to all her badness." She "believed that in her soul," she said; and she added also her opinion that Effie was "just hanging around to see if she could n't see our Ellen."

She was quite right. Effie's first interest in the adventure had worn off, and she was getting frightened; she tried to comfort herself by the assurance that as soon as it was all "found out" she would say, "I *told* her not to go!" She had a faint hope that Ellen's resolution had given out and she had returned, so sent a note over the "telegraph," which had often borne more harmful messages; but there was no answer. Then she grew angry; she said to herself that she hated Ellen. Thoroughly frightened, she felt a frantic desire to blame some one, so it was a comfort to see Lydia Wright walking sedately along the gravel path away from Mrs. Dale's front door.

Effie hailed her imperiously, but with some mystery in her manner. "Stop! I want to speak to you," she said.

It was half past two. Lydia, looking like a little clove pink in her white sunbonnet, which pressed her shining curls close against her round cheeks, had come over to say to Mrs. Dale, "Mother's love, and may Ellen come and spend the afternoon and take tea?" She stopped at Effie's command. "I came to invite Ellen to tea," she explained, nervously rolling the strings of her sunbonnet, " but Betsey Thomas says she is n't allowed to go out." Euphemia Temple had never seemed to Lydia more alarming.

"I guess Betsey Thomas does n't know what she's talking about! And I guess if you'd been nicer to Ellen it would n't have happened." Effie was almost in tears. Lydia was too astonished to defend herself or ask an explanation. " If you'll promise never to tell, I'll tell you something," Effie ended; "will you promise?"

"Yes," Lydia answered. " Only — don't."

Effie's imperative agitation terrified her so that her only thought was flight. "You've got to hear; it's your fault," Effie said sternly. " Promise you'll never tell?"

"I promise," said Lydia, shaking.

" Say, 'hope I may die if I do.'"

"'Hope I may die,'" Lydia stammered.

"*Ellen has run away!*"

Lydia gazed at her with horrified eyes, speechless.

"You promised not to tell," Effie threatened.

"I — I — I won't," said Lydia.

"Now go home!" cried Effie, with sudden rage. "If you 'd been nicer to her, she would n't have — It 's your fault!"

Lydia turned and fled, appalled at the news and at the responsibility of knowledge, but never doubting that she must keep her promise.

Effie, meantime, experienced no relief from her burst of confidence.

That there was something on her mind might have been guessed, had it not been that other members of the family seemed to have something on their minds, also; her aunt was nervous and absorbed; her mother plainly irritable.

"Everybody's crazy!" Effie declared, when Miss Dace assured her that she had never seen such a troublesome little girl; "everybody's crazy! You make such a fuss about your old declensions; and aunty says she is going down to mail a letter instead of sending Jim to do it, and coming out to play croquet with me; and mamma scolds if you look at her!"

"Why don't you go and see why Ellen wasn't here this morning?" Miss Dace suggested wearily.

"Oh, I hate everybody!" Effie responded, with angry irrelevance. Then she tried again to coax her aunt to play croquet.

"I can't, Effie, dear," Miss Jane said nervously. "I must go down to the post-office."

"You said that an hour ago; you could have mailed sixty letters by this time. Why don't you make Jim mail your old letter? or why don't you go, and come back? You just talk! Goodness!" said Effie, and stamped, for want of any better way of expressing her angry fright.

"Why *don't* I go?" Miss Jane said to herself. Her letter was stamped and addressed, though with nothing more definite as a direction than "Philadelphia." "There's nothing really personal in it," she reasoned, thinking of its contents. "I will mail it!" and she started for the village. She had done as much as start, early in the morning, but she had turned back, and the letter was still unmailed. "I'll wait and send it by the evening stage," she said. A dozen times that day, she put her hand into her pocket to destroy it, but each time she touched it she said, "No, there is no harm in sending it; and probably it won't reach him, anyhow. And if it did, it doesn't mean anything. No, there is no harm in sending it. But I won't mail it until to-night."

Four o'clock came, and Miss Jane Temple said to herself, "It must not go; I'll tear it up." She took the letter out and looked at it. "No, not yet. But I won't mail it; it would be foolish," she sighed to herself, "and it would never reach him."

Jane Temple's heart beat so fast that

she had a suffocated feeling, and went to the window for a breath of air. Effie was on the croquet ground. Miss Jane could hear the sharp click of the balls, as the child knocked them idly about. Somehow, the sight of Effie sent a wave of resolution to her heart. There was no reason why she should not send her letter, why she should not have a happiness of her own, have friends and interests of her own. "I have a right to my own life!" she said to herself again. She had a curious instant of something like hate for all this comfortable household. She opened the bottom drawer of the chest of drawers and took out the green crape shawl; as she touched it she felt suddenly courageous, and she put it over her shoulders with the thrill of one who buckles on his armor for a battle; and then she started for the post-office. Perhaps it was the green shawl lying like a vine upon her white dress that caught Effie's eye, for she ran across the lawn to her aunt's side.

"Why, you've got that horrid shawl on!" she commented. She had to say something disagreeable or burst into tears. "It's hideous!"

"Don't, Effie," said Miss Jane coldly, "don't hang on my hand that way."

"Where are you going? Oh, how horrid everything is!"

"To the village; you had better go and get dressed for tea."

"I'm going to the village with you."

Miss Jane was silent. She wished she could make Effie obey her, but she was too exhausted to try.

"Why don't you go to see Ellen?" she said; she made up her mind not to mail the letter in Effie's presence.

Effie opened her lips to reply, and then stopped and stamped her foot. "I — I — I hate her!" she said. The tears rushed to her eyes.

"Why, Effie! how can you speak so? Have you and Ellen quarreled? You should never say you hate any one."

"I hate, hate, *hate* her!" Effie sobbed, with all the pent-up fright of the day. "She's a bad, horrid girl; she's run away from home. Oh, my! isn't she wicked? I shouldn't think you'd want me to know such a girl."

Miss Jane Temple, with her fingers touching the letter in her pocket, stood still with astonishment. "What do you mean?"

"It isn't my fault. I told her not to. I said, 'Ellen, you oughtn't to run away.' And she was mad because I wouldn't go. She wanted me to run away, too! I wouldn't do such a thing. She's a dreadful girl! I don't want to live in this awful hole of an Old Chester when she comes back."

Miss Jane took Effie's hands from her face and held them in hers. "Tell me every single thing," she commanded. And Effie told her version.

And so it happened that it was nearly five o'clock before Miss Jane Temple, hurrying through the gardens, came to disturb the peace of the Dale household. She could not stop to mail the letter, and her pang of disappointment showed her how entirely she had meant to do it, despite all those hesitations.

Mrs. Dale had left her bedroom late in the afternoon; her head was better, but her heart ached. No word from Ellen! What should she do with this rebellious child? Her anxiety was full of self-examination. Wherein had she failed, that this extraordinary defiance was possible? She did not feel strong enough to read; nor could she put her mind upon anything except this present pain, which held in it all the pain of the past, all the old puzzle and despair. "*He* had this same persistency in doing what he knew was wrong," she was thinking; "my remonstrances only made things worse. Perhaps he would have been better without me? perhaps the child would be better without me! Oh, how can I meet my son in heaven, if I fail with Ellen!" Mrs. Dale's hands were lying idle in her lap, and her face was full of the old misery, and the new anxiety, when Miss Jane Temple came breathlessly through the hall, and stood a moment, hesitating, in the doorway.

"Mrs. Dale," she began, in an agitated voice, "I came to inquire about Ellen. Is she in her room? I"—

Mrs. Dale was annoyed. "Pray sit down, Jane. You are very good, I'm sure. Ellen has been troublesome, and I think it best for her to keep her room." She smiled formally. It was not the habit in Old Chester for one disciplinarian to criticise another; perhaps because they all followed the same methods.

"I am sorry to seem to intrude," said Miss Jane, her words broken with haste, "but Effie has just told me that — that — I fear you do not know Ellen's frame of mind — she — Effie"—

"My dear Jane," said Mrs. Dale, sitting up very straight, a little color coming into her face, "you are needlessly concerned. And Euphemia? You know in Old Chester a child's opinions are of no possible importance. I really think you make a mistake in encouraging her to talk."

"Oh, dear Mrs. Dale," Jane Temple burst out, "*Ellen has run away!*" Miss Jane was crying, and twisting her fingers together. "I'm sure it's all Effie's fault, but oh, what shall we do?"

"Ellen? Nonsense!" Mrs. Dale almost laughed. "Now, that comes of listening to Effie's talk. Really, it is a mistake. It has never been the practice in Old"—

"Indeed, I'm afraid something's wrong. Won't you send upstairs and see? Effie said she went away this morning at nine, and it's after five! Oh, do send upstairs and see!"

In spite of herself, Mrs. Dale felt suddenly apprehensive. "Of course, if you wish it. Will you touch that bell, if you please? But it is absurd. Your Euphemia might do such a thing, Jane Temple, but a child brought up in — Betsey Thomas, step upstairs, if you please, and tell Ellen that I say she may go out in the garden for a little walk before tea. Pray, Jane, control yourself; it is not proper that the child should see you so much agitated."

Miss Jane sank down upon the sofa, her breath coming quickly, and her eyes fixed upon the parlor door. Mrs. Dale waited in annoyed silence. Really, Euphemia Temple was a most objectionable child; this acquaintance must end at once. It occurred to her, with a vague comfort, that Ellen's naughtiness was owing to Effie's influence.

"I'm sorry to say it, Jane," she began majestically, "but I think I must not allow Ellen to see so much of Euphemia; Euphemia has been brought up so differently that"—

A door slammed in the upper hall, there was a rush downstairs, and Betsey Thomas bounced into the parlor. "She's not there! Ellen's not there!"

XIV

THE elderberry bushes under which Ellen had fallen asleep fringed a wide meadow. It had been mowed a week before, but when she awoke, the faint glow in the west where the sun had set, tinged its rough stubble and made it look as soft as though it were still deep with timothy grass. She sat up, stiff and tired, and wondering for a moment where she was. Oh, yes, she remembered. The peddler! She listened, breathless, for the sound of wheels and Edward's plodding step. But everything was still.

The yellow light behind the dark line of the hills was melting into violet dusk; the long shadows, which had stretched across the field when she first opened her eyes, were fading and fading into the great soft shadow of night. Everything seemed to be asleep, and she, of all the big world, awake. She listened, till her own pulses jarred the stillness. Not even a rustling leaf spoke beside her; the soundless dark held her in its centre. Then, suddenly, at her feet, a cricket chirped, and the silence, like a sphere of clear black glass, shivered and broke! She heard the grass where she had been lying lift itself with a brushing sound; she heard the snap of a twig under foot; she caught the soft nestling of some sleeping birds in the bushes behind her; the spell of silence was broken, and she drew a free breath. How late it was! The thought of her little bedroom flashed into her mind; her white bed, Betsey waiting to take the candle away; a wave of home-sickness made her feel faint. She must go home! she must run; it would soon be too dark to see where she was going.

But in that long, deep sleep she had lost her bearings. She started, keeping in the fields that skirted a road which led, she thought, to Old Chester; on and on she walked, farther and farther from home. Once or twice, coming upon a marsh or a wide shallow run, she turned into the road; but she ran then, quivering with fear until she could get back into the meadows, for there the tranquil hush of night did not frighten her. Once, a faint glitter in a dark pool caught her eye, and, glancing up through the birch-trees, she saw the moon looking at her between the leaves; after that, shadows began to grow out of the darkness, and the field glimmered like a silver shield; under the trees black caverns seemed to open and yawn; perhaps there were dragons in them! She instantly flew out into the open moonlight, her heart beating fiercely; she knew there were no dragons in the shadowy lairs, but that did not keep her from being horribly afraid of them. -After a while, walking on, well away from trees and bushes and shadows, she grew less frightened; she became vaguely conscious of the companionship of the kind, silent earth, with its intimate sky clasping it like a dark hand jeweled by the moon and stars. A sense of comfort and security came over her, — an ebbing of identity; fear and penitence fell away from her like heavy weights. It was as though the little human creature vibrated with the sonorous rhythmic march of the whole, and could not know so small a thing as self.

Once she lay down, and looked up into the clear moon-flooded depths, and into the broad kind face of the moon itself. She thought that children who could lie on their mothers' knees must feel as she did, now, lying here in the warm still fields, lying on the earth's friendly lap, safe, and warm, and cared for, swinging among the stars! she was sure she should be taken care of; she wondered, with not too keen an interest, what the moon was saying to the listening earth? She sighed with comfort. It seemed to her that she would never get up, but lie here, like a little mound, that would melt somehow into the field and the grass. Perhaps it was the pagan in the child, this instinct for the Great Mother; very simply, without knowing why, there in the silence and peace she knelt down and laid her cheek against the earth, and kissed it softly. Then she rose and trudged on in the moonlight.

But suddenly she was stung into alertness; a house loomed up ahead of her. Then, instantly, she was afraid! Her heart pounded as, giving one flying look of terror over her shoulder, she ran towards it. A picket fence inclosed the farmhouse from its wider garden, making that small dooryard which country people love. Ellen had a glimpse of the room within: a woman beside a table, sewing; a man stretched out in a rocking-chair, asleep; the top of a cradle rocking drowsily to and fro. It was not an especially attractive interior, but it was human, and seeing it, Ellen knew once more that she was disobedient and desolate, and with her self-knowledge came back the misery which she had lost in the fields. The hope of being protected and taken home made the weary child sob with joy. She lifted the latch of the gate, when, suddenly, a dog barked! Ellen's heart stood still; she tried to cry out, but her voice was so husky with fear that it did not seem to be hers. That was a terrible moment. A strange voice from her own lips? Who was she? A beggar at a farmer's gate, nothing to eat, no place to sleep, and a dog barking at her! She heard the creature running, bounding towards her from the farther side of the house, and she turned and flew back towards the road. The steps followed her, and a quick volley of barks, and then a threatening growl. Ellen sobbed aloud as she ran; it seemed to her that she could not breathe, and the dog was close upon her, she thought. She caught her foot, and fell headlong on the rough stubble. She was too exhausted to rise. Every instant she thought she would feel the dog's breath on her neck; but he did not come. Yet it was some moments before she had the courage or the strength to rise. She had bruised her knee on the stiff, newly-mown grass, and it hurt her, which gave her the relief of a new misery.

She started again, still keeping in the fields, and walked nearly a mile before she saw another light gleam out. She stopped and looked at it. There was a barn near the road, and some haystacks, and a stone's-throw up on the hillside the big balconied farmhouse, with the light in the window; it stood at the top of its grape-trellised terraces, with its flagged pavement under the lowest balcony, and its comfortable Dutch exterior inviting her.

How the child longed to go and knock at the door! But she only stood and looked at it with anguished eyes. The remembrance of the dog was too dreadful to let her think for a moment of going any nearer, and yet she could not go quite away. She wondered if a dog at the house could hear her breathing down here by the barn? As she looked towards the spot of cheerful light, it went out. That meant that the farmer and his wife had gone to bed; the house was perfectly dark. Ellen turned and looked at the barn; she might go in there? If she could once get in, no dog could hurt her. The cows and horses seemed like friends to the desolate child. But when, very softly, she put her hands on the big doors, she found they were barred on the inside; she heard a long-drawn sigh from within, and a muffled stamp. Oh, how comfortable they were, the cows and horses! She leaned her cheek against the door for a long time, and listened; she could not bear to go away from these friendly creatures and be alone again. Once or twice she caught the soft, deep breaths, and once she heard a horse biting at his crib, and a cow striking her horns against the stanchions. But after a while she remembered the haystacks behind the barn, and thought she would go to one of them and rest a little, and then, if she could get her courage up to the point of going off alone into the night, start once more for home.

It took some minutes to reach the yard behind the barn, for she stopped at every step to listen, but once there, she was glad to sit down and lean against the soft, sweet hay of one of the stacks; she even dug out a little shelter for herself, and cuddled into the small hole to keep warm, for the August chill had crept into the night.

The full, still pour of the moon filled the barnyard with vaporous light, in which the shadow of the haystack lay like a black pool. The pain of fright still gripped Ellen's heart; and when she noticed that the pasture in front of her was bare and free from rocks, and thought that it would be a good place for fairies to dance, she banished the fancy, with the assertion that she must say her prayers; perhaps God would take care of her if she said her prayers, but if she thought about fairies He might be angry.

"Now I lay me down to sleep,"

she began to repeat rapidly, squeezing her eyes tight shut,

"I pray the Lord my soul to keep;
If I should die before I wake,
I pray the Lord my soul to take.

"God bless grandmother, and make me a good girl"—then all the little form which she had used ever since she knew how to speak. It meant nothing to Ellen; the kiss in the field had said it all.

As she grew warmer here in the hay, fatigue blurred her fear. Vague thoughts of the fairies came unchallenged to her mind, and dim recollections of her old life, lived so long, long ago: her grandmother's step on the stairs while she had been waiting to escape to the summerhouse to meet Effie. Effie? Why, she had forgotten her! It had all happened so long ago. Yesterday? The word had no meaning to her. Then she drifted into thoughts of the garden, and the sunshine, and the hollyhock ladies; she remembered the little teas on the side porch when her grandmother had allowed her to invite Lydia, and had had cakes baked to fit her small dishes; yes, she and Lydia had played together long, long ago; they used to meet by the poplar-trees, or swing, and talk, and watch the horse-hairs turning into snakes. Suddenly, the ache and misery of homesickness surged up in that spot below the breastbone where the soul seems to suffer. Ellen cried hopelessly; she could not imagine that she should ever be at home again.

The pool of shadow in front of the haystack lessened, rippling back and back like a falling tide. The moon had climbed up behind the barn, and began to peer over the shoulder of the stack; she had not the same expression she had worn in the fields; her face seemed smaller, and she looked coldly down on the child's grief. Ellen pulled out some more hay and burrowed farther into her little shelter.

Into the midst of her hopelessness came the sound of a wagon rattling along the road. Ellen saw the light of a swinging lantern, and heard voices, but no words. "It must be *robbers!*" she thought, pressing in against the hay to hide herself. It never occurred to her that it might be some one searching for her.

After a while she slept, and then awoke with a start. There was a soft, slow step in the barnyard. The pool of shadow before her had ebbed quite away; the indifferent moon was going down, sinking behind the hill; there was a mist lying like white gauze over the ground. Again that step, and the strange, shuffling noise. Ellen hardly dared breathe; It was not like a dog. All was quiet for a few moments, and then, — again! Something seemed to loom up in the misty darkness, something big and black; something which sighed, close to Ellen's face! Perhaps the child fainted for a moment in her ghastly fright, for there seemed to be a gap of vacancy; and then she knew that it was a cow, whose gentle and astonished eyes had looked into hers, and who had drawn back with a frightened snort.

After that Ellen was awake for a long time; the moon had quite gone, and all the world was wrapped in crystal dark. The cow did not disturb her again, although she heard the big creature moving about. Once, far off, a dog barked. "There *must* be robbers!" she said to herself, growing cold with fear. Then everything was still, until from some distant farm came, faint and thin, through the darkness, a cock-crow.

Ellen thought with a leap of her heart that it must be nearly morning; but the night still pressed close about her. Oh, would it never end? Again she slept, and again awoke with a start.

The sun was up; above the hill the sky rippled with small white clouds, and then soared into an arc of smiling blue. The barnyard was full of chickens, and there were four cows standing about, chewing their cud, and waiting to be milked; but right in front of her, staring, open-mouthed, was a boy in blue overalls, with a bucket of foaming milk in each hand. He had no hat on, and his shock of pale hair seemed to be standing on end with astonishment.

"Oh, may I have a drink of milk?" said Ellen. She sat up, gazing with anguished expectancy at the milk. The boy nodded, without speaking; he put down one bucket, and lifted the other to the child's lips. Her hands were trembling with weakness, and she sobbed as she drank. She did not let go of the bucket when she stopped for breath; and then she drank again. "Oh, sir, I've no money," she said, "but" —

"Who are you?" the boy interrupted. "Are you the little girl that's lost from Old Chester?"

"May I have a little more milk?" the child entreated. "My grandmother'll pay you. Oh, *grandmother!*"

"If you come up to the house, they'll give ye some breakfast," said the boy, his eyes big with excitement. "You're the girl, I know you are!" As he spoke he tilted the bucket for her to drink. "You come on up to the house, now. Don't let on who you are, till I tell 'em."

"Oh, no, I'm going home; oh, I'm very much obliged to you, but I'm going home," said Ellen, rising, and beginning, with unsteady hands, to brush the hay from her hair and dress.

"No, you ain't," said the boy firmly, "not till I've told the boss; now you just wait here." With that he picked up his buckets, and walked swiftly in the direction of the house. When, ten minutes later, he came running back with a big grizzled farmer, the little nest in the hay was empty.

XV

THE night which had brought such experiences to Ellen had been full of dismay and pain to her friends. Perhaps no one suffered more keenly than did poor little Lydia, lying awake with her dreadful secret. At ten, her mother found her staring into the darkness, and sobbing now and then, under her breath.

"Tell mother what is the matter, Lydia," said Mrs. Wright, who had been careful not to let the child know of the anxiety concerning Ellen. But Lydia had promised "not to tell," and she kept her word. Effie, however, having given her information, and assured everybody who would listen to her, half a dozen times

over, that she had "told Ellen not to,"
— Effie was calmly sleeping. Messengers were hurried in every direction. Miss Jane Temple stayed with Mrs. Dale until almost midnight, trying to emulate her calmness, but seeing the elder woman's face grow white and haggard as the slow hours found Ellen still away from home. Betsey Thomas's grief was unfeigned, and her anger at herself, Mrs. Dale, Effie Temple, and the peddler — who had by that time appeared and told all he knew — expended itself in sharp words about every one but Ellen; for the real offender she had nothing but incoherent expressions of affection and of praise. Mrs. Dale was silent. What her thoughts, her self-reproaches, her most honest and vindicating judgments may have been no one knew; not even Miss Jane, sitting beside her as the night wore on. At dawn she lost her pain in an hour's restless sleep, and by that time, fleeing from the boy who had given her the milk, Ellen was

walking swiftly in the direction of her home. This was really only a fortunate chance, for the child had been so turned around, in all these experiences, that she had no idea where Old Chester lay. Once she dared to stop a man who was driving a clattering and clanging mowing-machine along the road, to ask him if she were near Old Chester, only to be shocked to learn that she was twelve or fourteen miles away.

"I'm goin' a good piece in that direction," he said, slowly, neither speculation nor kindness in his stolid harmless face; "I got a field to mow; an' you kin stand up here in front of me, if you want to."

Ellen was only too glad to avail herself of his aid. Her mind was fastened with such intensity upon the idea of getting home that she felt no fear of the mowing-machine or even of a strange man; had it been the peddler who made this offer, she would have accepted it! This concentration kept her silent; she volunteered no information about herself, and the man asked no questions. When at last he drew his horses up before a lane into which he must turn to reach the field to be mowed, he only said, briefly, "Yer not more 'n nine miles off now, sissy." And Ellen said, "Yes, sir; thank you," and plodded on alone.

She passed several people after that, and one or two carts, but no one offered her a ride; one man drew up his horse and looked at her curiously, and seemed about to speak, but Ellen's resolute little face, set towards Old Chester, seemed to satisfy him that she could not be the lost child of whom he had heard rumors an hour before. It seemed to Ellen, having wakened at five, that it must be at least twelve when she sat down by the roadside to rest; but really it was only half past eight, and a traveler who had gotten off a train at Mercer three hours before had had ample time to walk leisurely along in the direction of Old Chester and overtake her. Ellen, dozing with fatigue, opened her eyes to see this traveler standing before her. He had a stick over his shoulder, on which he had slung a traveling-bag. He was a little man, with anxious eyes and a timid air.

"Why, it *can't* be little Ellen!" he said.

Ellen stared at him, her eyes dull with misery, and then a flash of recognition sent the blood surging into her face, and she burst out into passionate crying.

Mr. Tommy Dove lifted the stick from his shoulder and rested his bag carefully on the ground.

"Why, little Ellen Dale! there, — there, don't, my dear, don't! Where is your grandmother, or Betsey Thomas? Are you alone, little Ellen? There, now, there!"

"Oh, Mr. Tommy!" the child said, "Oh, take me home; won't you *please* take me home?" Mr. Tommy, distressed almost to tears, looked this way and that for aid, while he tried to comfort her. "Yes, my little girl; yes, yes; directly! You shall go home directly. But how did you come here? Where is — anybody? You are not alone, little Ellen?"

"I'll — I'll tell you — about it," she said, trying to speak, but shaken by these long pent up tears; "I'll tell you all about it, if you'll *just* take me home. Oh, Mr. Tommy, I ran away, — I ran away from home!" The poor child rocked back and forth, and moaned in unchildlike grief. As for Mr. Dove, he was so far from a proper perception of discipline that he took the little penitent into his arms, and said, "Well, there! that's no matter; it's all right — it's all right. Why, I've done it myself!" said Mr. Dove. But Ellen had reached at last that clear-sighted repentance which knows excuses to be false and weak, and will none of them — the only repentance which has power to turn the sinner from darkness to light. "Oh — no — " she said, faintly;

"I'm a bad, bad girl. Maybe God will forgive me some day, but grandmother never can," wailed Ellen, with no knowledge of sarcasm, but realizing instinctively how much harder it is to make one's peace with one's kind than with Infinite Goodness; and then she tried to tell her story: "Effie Temple was going to run away with me. But she was better than I was; she wouldn't. She said Miss Jane wanted her to have a dress fitted, and — and so I came by myself; and won't you please take me home? Oh, I want to go home!"

"Yes, yes, yes, my dear," Mr. Tommy soothed her. "There, we'll go right home now. And — and you say Miss Jane is still in Old Chester? Well, I knew it; I thought so; but — I made up my mind to come back. It was weak to stay away." Apparently Mr. Tommy was still weak, for the color came and went painfully in his elderly face. "And is her brother there, too?" he questioned.

"Dick?" said Ellen, wiping her eyes. "Oh, no, he went away a good while ago."

"I meant"—explained the other, "I referred to—to Mr. Temple; *her* brother."

"Oh, yes, he's there. Effie said her papa loved her, and so she wouldn't run away. But my grandmother does love me, so she does. At least, she did. She won't any more; oh, never any more!"

Mr. Dove seemed to reflect; he took off his hat, and then put it on again, thoughtfully. "We must get a conveyance," he announced. As he spoke, a woman with a basket on her arm passed, and then looked back at Ellen.

"Are you the little girl that was lost?" she said, pausing.

"I—ran away," Ellen answered truthfully, hanging her head with shame.

"She's just going home, ma'am, now," Mr. Dove broke in, his mild voice full of comfort and sympathy. "Can you tell me where I can hire a vehicle of any kind?"

The woman considered. "There's the Smith farm, a little piece up the road; guess they'd lend you their carryall?"

Mr. Tommy hurried in the direction the woman had indicated, leaving Ellen to her care, and returning in a surprisingly short time with a battered and dusty carriage drawn by a lively young sorrel horse. There was a boy with him, who would, Mr. Tommy explained, bring the carryall back again.

Ellen was glad to creep into it; her eyes were downcast and her cheeks burning with shame, for the questions the woman had asked her during Mr. Dove's absence opened up depths of mortification of which she had never dreamed. Her despair had been too dreadful for the smaller pain of mortification. But now she bent her head down sidewise and looked out at the fields past which the sorrel horse was hurrying them at a fine rate; she supposed Mr. Tommy would ask the same dreadful questions. But Mr. Tommy seemed as conscious and embarrassed as she. He made no reference to her wickedness, and was silent so long that Ellen grew tremulous with apprehension; his reproof, when it came, would be terrible, she thought, cowering.

"I recollect," he said at last, coughing a little behind his hand, "I recollect Miss Effie Temple; she is Her niece."

Ellen drew a long breath. To talk about Effie was a respite. "Yes, sir," she said vaguely; and then she saw a sign-post that said, "Old Chester, 7 miles," and she felt, through all her relief at going home, a sudden sinking of the heart that was almost sickness.

"Miss Effie did not, I think, like me," Mr. Tommy observed. "I did not notice it at first; she was only a little girl, so I did not notice it. But, upon reflection, I felt that she did not. I felt that she was glad when — I was called away from Old Chester."

Ellen made an effort to seem interested

in spite of the misery tugging at her heart. "But Miss Jane was sorry, Mr. Tommy, when you went away. Effie told me so."

Mr. Tommy started; he put his hand upon the door-knob. "Oh, no, no, little Ellen; you are mistaken. I think perhaps I'll not proceed to Old Chester. His voice wavered so that Ellen gazed at him in astonishment.

"Why, Effie said so, Mr. Tommy," she assured him; and then the connection in which Effie had said it came back to Ellen's mind, and the child blushed as violently as Mr. Tommy himself.

The apothecary, however, struggled to regain his composure. "Yes, yes, I see. Always kind, always kind. Yes, I understand. Sorry? of course;—for me. But I believe I am not ready to come back — yet. I'll — I'll wait a little longer; I find it is difficult to return. I — I think"—

"Are n't you going to take me home, Mr. Tommy?" Ellen interposed, alarmed at the prospect of being dropped by the roadside. Mr. Tommy drew a long breath.

"I'll take you home, little Ellen; yes, I'll do that; no harm to do that. But you don't understand. No, you couldn't understand; and yet, I have sometimes thought that the other child did."

"Effie?" said Ellen boldly. "She knew all about it, Mr. Tommy. She said Miss Jane was mad because you went away. She thought you'd come back, Effie said; but you didn't, and she was mad. Are you going back now, Mr. Tommy?"

Mr. Dove fell into the corner of the carriage, too deep in thought to answer her.

"Three miles to Old Chester," a signboard declared, and Ellen forgot Mr. Tommy's interests in her own. Twice they were stopped by excited voices hailing them from the roadside.

"Oh, there she is!" "Oh, where were you, child? How did you get lost?" And when the first relief and excitement had been expressed, came astonished exclamations that it was Mr. Tommy who had brought the lost child home.

"Hallo, hallo!" said one man; "did you find her, Tommy, or did she find you?" He was glad to be facetious to hide his agitation. Ellen had made a sensation in Old Chester.

Once they stopped long enough to let Miss Minns climb on to the carriage step and give Ellen a sounding kiss. Miss Minns was the postmistress, and was tall and pale, and had the reputation of being cross. But now she was almost as gentle as Miss Jane Temple, except in her shrill surprise upon seeing who was escorting the lost child.

By this time Ellen could scarcely sit still. "Oh, grandmother, grandmother!" she was whispering to herself. At Mrs. Dale's gate, Mr. Tommy made a gesture to the lad who was driving them.

"Boy," he said, "you can stop. Here's your money. I shall get out here, little Ellen, but he will drive you on."

Mr. Dove got out of the carryall as he spoke, but Ellen instantly followed him. "I'd rather walk with you, Mr. Tommy," she said in a frightened voice. And then, a moment later with wildly beating hearts, the apothecary and the child found themselves standing before the great iron gates of Mrs. Dale's garden.

Beyond, a little farther up the lane, was Mr. Henry Temple's place. Mr. Tommy looked towards it with a wistful sort of fright, and yet a quiet dignity too; for Thomas Dove, as Mrs. Dale had said, had seen something of the world since that miserable night when Henry Temple ordered him from his house. Even as he looked Mr. Temple's gate swung open, and Miss Jane came with hurrying, anxious steps down the road. She was hastening to Mrs. Dale's, hoping that she might hear some tidings of Ellen.

Mr. Tommy, fumbling with the clanging iron latch of the gate, looked about him a little wildly, as though uncertain in which direction to flee; but Ellen turned, with a cry. "Oh, Miss Jane, I'm here. Oh, where's grandmother?"

Miss Jane, with eyes only for Ellen, ran towards them and caught the little girl in her arms; "Oh— *Ellen!*" she said, her kind eyes running over. And then she looked up to see who had brought the child back.

"What! Mr. Dove!" Jane Temple put out her hand, and then turned away, and then looked back again. "Run, Ellen, run to your grandmother, my dear," she said faintly. But Ellen had not waited to be told. She slipped from Miss Jane's arms, and ran as fast as she could towards that distressed and anxious house where, worn from the night, Mrs. Dale was waiting and praying for tidings of the one human creature that she loved. Ellen, blind with tears, went stumbling up the front steps, and saw, within the darkened parlor, the figure of her grandmother pacing with insistent composure, up and down, up and down. How she reached her, how her little heart found words, how the agony of all those hours ended, the child never knew.

As for Miss Jane, she seemed to waver, as she stood there in the morning sunshine before her old lover; should she go or stay? should she follow Ellen — or her heart?

"Oh, Mr. Dove!" she said, breathing quickly, and looking away from him, but feeling his eyes commanding hers, and so looking back at him again, — "Oh, Mr. Dove! I have n't seen you this summer. Are you well?" The night of anxiety had been too great a strain; her self-possession was gone. "I hope you are very well," she repeated, much agitated. She put her hand in her pocket, and seemed to crush something with nervous haste.

Perhaps her agitation calmed Mr. Tommy. He took her left hand and held it in his. "I felt I must come back. May I stay, Miss Jane? Will you let me stay?

You will not say I must go away again? We have our own lives to live; please tell me I may stay, ma'am? Oh, I hope you're not angry that I have come back?"

"Angry?" said Miss Jane, her lips trembling and her eyes smiling. "Oh, why should I be, Mr. Dove? Why — I" — There was a crumpled letter in her hand, and she put it up to her face to hide her tears, and then laid it in his hands, with a gesture as lovely and as impulsive as a girl's. "I'm glad you've come back; you must never leave me any more!"

They had both forgotten Ellen.

Books of Fiction

William Henry Bishop.
Detmold: A Romance. 18mo, $1.25.
The House of a Merchant Prince. 12mo, $1.50.
Choy Susan, and other Stories. 16mo, $1.25.
The Golden Justice. 16mo, $1.25; paper, 50 cents.

E. W. Howe.
A Man Story. 12mo, $1.50.
The Mystery of the Locks. New Edition. 16mo, $1.25.
The Story of a Country Town. New Edition. 16mo, $1.25; paper, 50 cents.
A Moonlight Boy. With Portrait of the Author. 12mo, $1.50; paper, 50 cents.

Round-Robin Series.
Each volume, 16mo, $1.00; paper, 50 cents.
Damen's Ghost.
Madame Lucas.
Leone.
Doctor Ben.
The Strike in the B—— Mill.
Fanchette. *Cloth only.*
Dorothea. *Cloth only.*

Ellen Olney Kirk.
Ciphers. 16mo, $1.25.
The Story of Margaret Kent. New Edition. 16mo, $1.25; paper, 50 cents.
Sons and Daughters. 12mo, $1.25; paper, 50 cents.
Queen Money. New Edition. 16mo, $1.25; paper, 50 cents.
Better Times. Stories. 12mo, $1.50.
A Midsummer Madness. 16mo, $1.25; paper, 50 cents.
A Lesson in Love. 16mo, $1.00; paper, 50 cents.
A Daughter of Eve. 12mo, $1.50; paper, 50 cents.
Walford. 16mo, $1.25; paper, 50 cents.

HOUGHTON, MIFFLIN & CO., Publishers.

Books of Fiction

Hans Christian Andersen.
Works. In ten uniform volumes, 12mo, each $1.00; the set, $10.00; half calf, $25.00.
In ten uniform volumes, 12mo, each $1.00; the set, $10.00; half calf, $25.00.
The Improvisatore; or, Life in Italy.
The Two Baronesses.
O. T.; or, Life in Denmark.
Only a Fiddler.
In Spain and Portugal.
A Poet's Bazaar. A Picturesque Tour.
Pictures of Travel.
The Story of my Life. With Portrait.
Wonder Stories told for Children. Illustrated.
Stories and Tales. Illustrated.

Mrs. James A. Field.
High-Lights. 16mo, $1.25.

Blanche Willis Howard.
One Summer. New *Popular Edition*. Illustrated by Hoppin. 16mo, $1.25.
Aulnay Tower. 12mo, $1.50; paper, 50 cents.
Aunt Serena. 16mo, $1.25; paper, 50 cents.
Guenn. Illustrated. 12mo, $1.50; paper, 50 cents.
The Open Door. Crown 8vo, $1.50; paper, 50 cents.
A Fellowe and His Wife. Collaborated by Blanche Willis Howard and William Sharp. 16mo, $1.25.

Rossiter Johnson (editor).
Little Classics. 18mo, each, $1.00. The set, in box, $18.00; half calf, or half morocco, $35.00.

1. Exile.
2. Intellect.
3. Tragedy.
4. Life.
5. Laughter.
6. Love.
7. Romance.
8. Mystery.
9. Comedy.
10. Childhood.
11. Heroism.
12. Fortune.
13. Narrative Poems.
14. Lyrical Poems.
15. Minor Poems.
16. Nature.
17. Humanity.
18. Authors.

Virginia W. Johnson.
The House of the Musician. 16mo, paper, 50 cents.

HOUGHTON, MIFFLIN & CO., Publishers.

Books of Fiction

Jane G. Austin.
A Nameless Nobleman. 16mo, $1.25; paper, 50 cents.
The Desmond Hundred. 16mo, $1.00; paper, 50 cents.
Standish of Standish. 16mo, $1.25.
Doctor LeBaron and His Daughters. 16mo, $1.25.
Betty Alden. 16mo, $1.25.

Edwin Lassetter Bynner.
Agnes Surriage. 12mo, $1.50; paper, 50 cents.
Penelope's Suitors. 24mo, boards, 50 cents.
Damen's Ghost. 16mo, $1.00; paper, 50 cents.

Helen Campbell.
Under Green Apple-Boughs. Illustrated 16mo, paper, 50 cents.

Harford Flemming.
A Carpet Knight. 16mo, $1.25.

Oliver Wendell Holmes.
Elsie Venner. New *Riverside Edition*. Crown 8vo, $1.50.
The Same. 16mo, paper, 50 cents.
The Guardian Angel. New *Riverside Edition*. Crown 8vo, $1.50.
The Same. 16mo, paper, 50 cents.
A Mortal Antipathy. First Opening of the New Portfolio. New *Riverside Edition*. Crown 8vo, gilt top, $1.50.
My Hunt after "The Captain," etc. Illustrated. 32mo, 75 cents.

HOUGHTON, MIFFLIN & CO., Publishers.

Books of Fiction

Sarah Orne Jewett.

The King of Folly Island, and other People. 16mo, $1.25.

Tales of New England. In Riverside Aldine Series. 16mo, $1.00.

A White Heron, and other Stories. 18mo, gilt top, $1.25.

A Marsh Island. 16mo, $1.25; paper, 50 cents.

A Country Doctor. 16mo, $1.25.

Deephaven. 18mo, gilt top, $1.25.

Old Friends and New. 18mo, gilt top, $1.25.

Country By-Ways. 18mo, gilt top, $1.25.

The Mate of the Daylight, and Friends Ashore. 18mo, gilt top, $1.25.

Betty Leicester. 18mo, gilt top, $1.25.

Strangers and Wayfarers. 16mo, $1.25.

William Makepeace Thackeray.

Complete Works. *Illustrated Library Edition.* Including two newly compiled volumes, containing material not hitherto collected in any American or English Edition. With Biographical and Bibliographical Introductions, Portrait, and over 1600 Illustrations. 22 vols. crown 8vo, gilt top, each, $1.50. The set, $33.00; half calf, $60.50; half calf, gilt top, $65.00; half levant, $77.00.

1. Vanity Fair. I.
2. Vanity Fair. II; Lovel the Widower.
3. Pendennis. I.
4. Pendennis. II.
5. Memoirs of Yellowplush, etc.
6. Burlesques.
7. History of Samuel Titmarsh, etc.
8. Barry Lyndon and Denis Duval.
9. The Newcomes. I.
10. The Newcomes. II.
11. Paris Sketch Book, etc.
12. Irish Sketch Book, etc.
13. The Four Georges, etc.
14. Henry Esmond.
15. The Virginians. I.
16. The Virginians. II.
17. Philip. I.
18. Philip. II.; Catherine.
19. Roundabout Papers, etc.
20. Christmas Stories, etc.
21. Contributions to Punch, etc.
22. Miscellaneous Essays.

Thackeray's Lighter Hours. Selections from Thackeray. With Portrait. 32mo, 75 cents.

HOUGHTON, MIFFLIN & CO., Publishers.

www.ingramcontent.com/pod-product-compliance
Lightning Source LLC
Chambersburg PA
CBHW021810230426
43669CB00008B/697